THE
SUBTLE RULES
THE DENSE

A SERIES BY

Phoebe Collings-James

WITH TEXTS BY

SERAFINE1369

Rehana Zaman

& Kathryn Yusoff

THE SUBTLE RULES THE DENSE

ABOUT
THE SUBTLE
RULES THE
DENSE

Moulded from clay, between 2021 and 2023, *The subtle rules the dense* is a series of ceramic chest plates, by the artist Phoebe Collings-James. The works, first made during Collings-James' participation in the Freelands Lomax Ceramics Fellowship at Camden Arts Centre in 2021, were inspired by encounters with Makonde and Yoruba body masks and the anatomical armour of the Roman muscle cuirass in exhibitions and antique dealers' windows. Collings-James was drawn to the objects and way in which their ritualistic and often brutal histories sat at odds with their contemporary presentation as ornamental fetish objects. For Collings-James, *The subtle rules the dense* is an extension and exploration of these lineages, each work a new relic holding uncertain futures as well as histories of violence and ritual.

This series was first exhibited at Camden Arts Centre in *A Scratch! A Scratch!*, the title of which alludes to both the sgraffito techniques used in Collings-James' ceramics and the death of Mercutio in William Shakespeare's *Romeo and Juliet*, and more specifically Harold Perrineau's magical, queer, vulnerable Mercutio in Baz Luhrmann's 1996 film adaptation of the play. In this volume, SERAFINE1369 writes of the film's influence on Collings-James and themself; it "made a mark on both of us [...] as teenagers, a slick and gaudy celebration of the tragedy of falling in love. Or something". [1]

1. SERAFINE1369, pg. 45

2. William Shakespeare, *Romeo and Juliet*, c.1595. Act III, Scene I.

"A plague o' both your houses! They have made worms' meat of me". [2] In Mercutio's death, we see the subtle as it intersects with the dense, the queer magic of his character tied to, then cut from, the dense matter of his bloody, visceral earthy body. Collings-James pulled the title *The subtle rules the dense* from *Meditations on the Tarot: A Journey into Christian Hermeticism*, an esoteric Christian exploration of Tarot cards, published anonymously in the 20th century. It's through the lens of tarot, the spiritual and the subtle that artist Rehana Zaman accesses Phoebe Collings-James' work in *note to a future self, an artwork in motion, horse.* Excerpts from the Quran, the King James' Bible and Marcella Kroll's *Nature Nurture Oracle Deck* emerge through descriptions of Collings-James' studio and the clay-laden soil in Walthamstow, "'heavy soil' – difficult to manage, fertile if handled 'the right way'".[3]

3. Rehana Zaman, pg. 53

Clay has been one of the central media in Collings-James' practice since discovering ceramics at a Nuove artist residency in Italy. For Collings-James, the appeal of working with clay is in the physical sensation; clay is a seductive material, in both its plastic and fired 'finished' form. In *The subtle rules the dense*, the dense is the physical materiality of existence – blood, clay, viscera – but also our clumsy signifiers of race, class, sexuality and genders, and how awkwardly or disobediently we may wear them. In 2022, several pieces from the series were exhibited at Two Temple Place and York Art Gallery as a part of the group exhibition *Body Vessel Clay*. The exhibition explored clay's haptic, malleable and metaphoric potential, whilst tracing post-colonial, gender and class perspectives on ceramics' manufacture and ownership across continents. In their conversation at Beaconsfield Gallery, transcribed in this publication, Collings-James and Professor Kathryn Yusoff discuss *A Billion Black Anthropocenes or None*, Yusoff's 2019 transdisciplinary essay on black feminist theory, geography and earth sciences. Clay, rock and the materiality of geology are inseparable from the extractive politics in which we live and work; "rock doesn't exist in a vacuum — it is in relation to water, air and people and touch…"[4] Collings-James says of visiting a clay mine in Cornwall.

4. Phoebe Collings-James, pg. 73

5. Aimé Cesaire, *Return to My Native Land*, 1956.

"Red earth, blood earth, blood brother earth",[5] a quote from post-colonial poet and politician Aimé Césaire, can be found both in Yusoff's writing and scrawled across Collings-James' chest plates, in calligraphic incisions. This publication brings together a series of disparate responses to *The subtle rules the dense*, reflecting the nuanced and ambiguous nature of Collings-Jame's work. The chest plates defy categorisation; at once masculine and feminine; pregnant Makonde body masks and muscular Roman armour; soft malleable clay and strong vitrified rock. "All magic, including sorcery, is the putting into practice of this: that the subtle rules the dense".[6]

6. Anon., *Mediations on the Tarot: A Journey into Christian Hermeticism*, 1967.

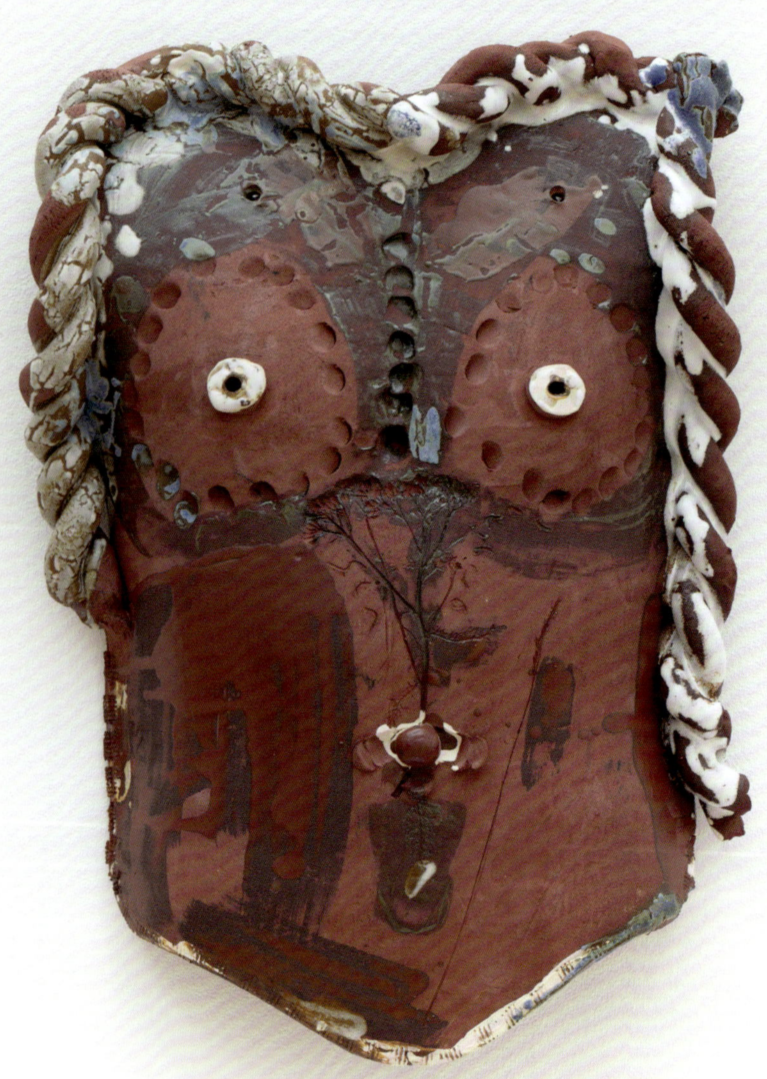

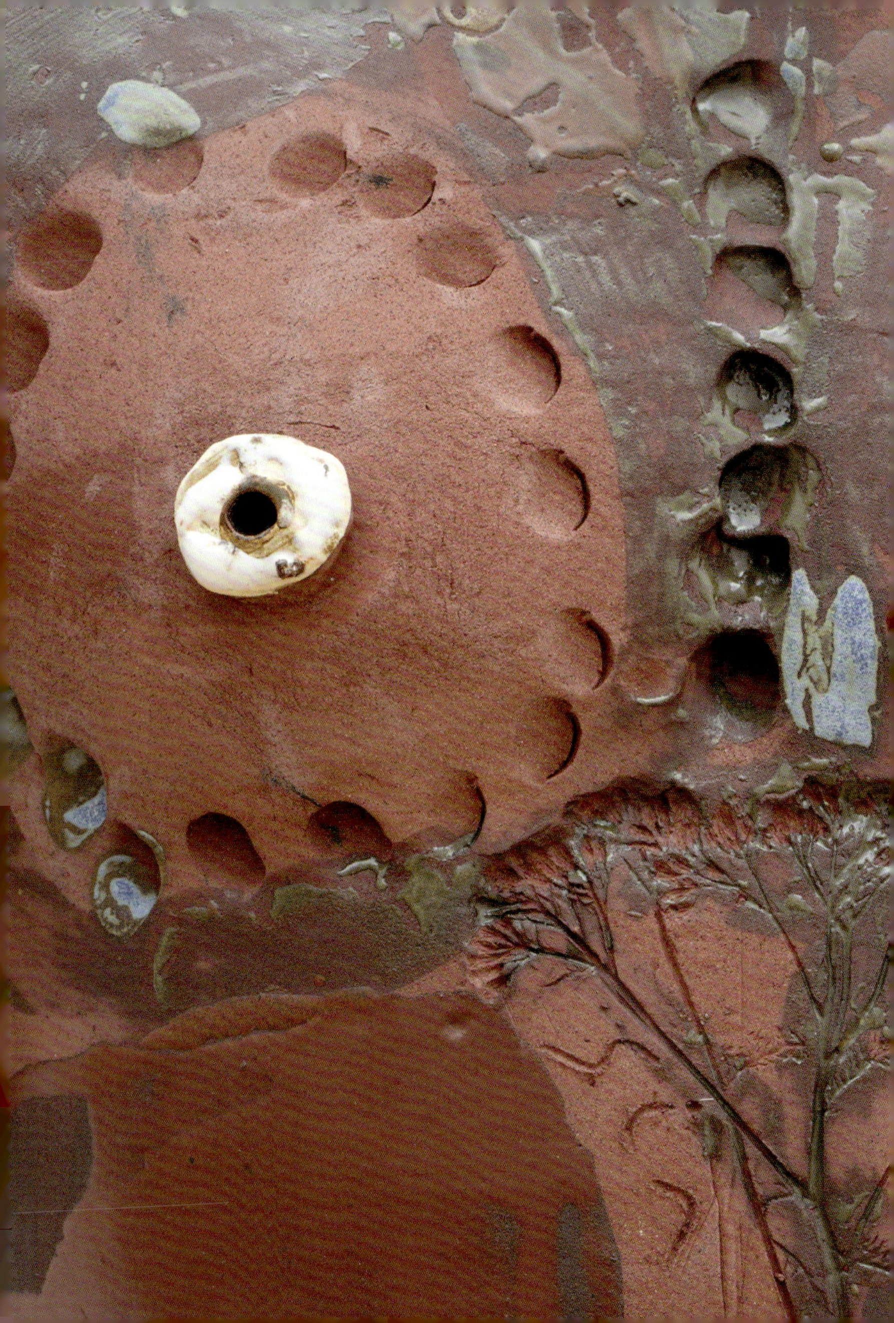

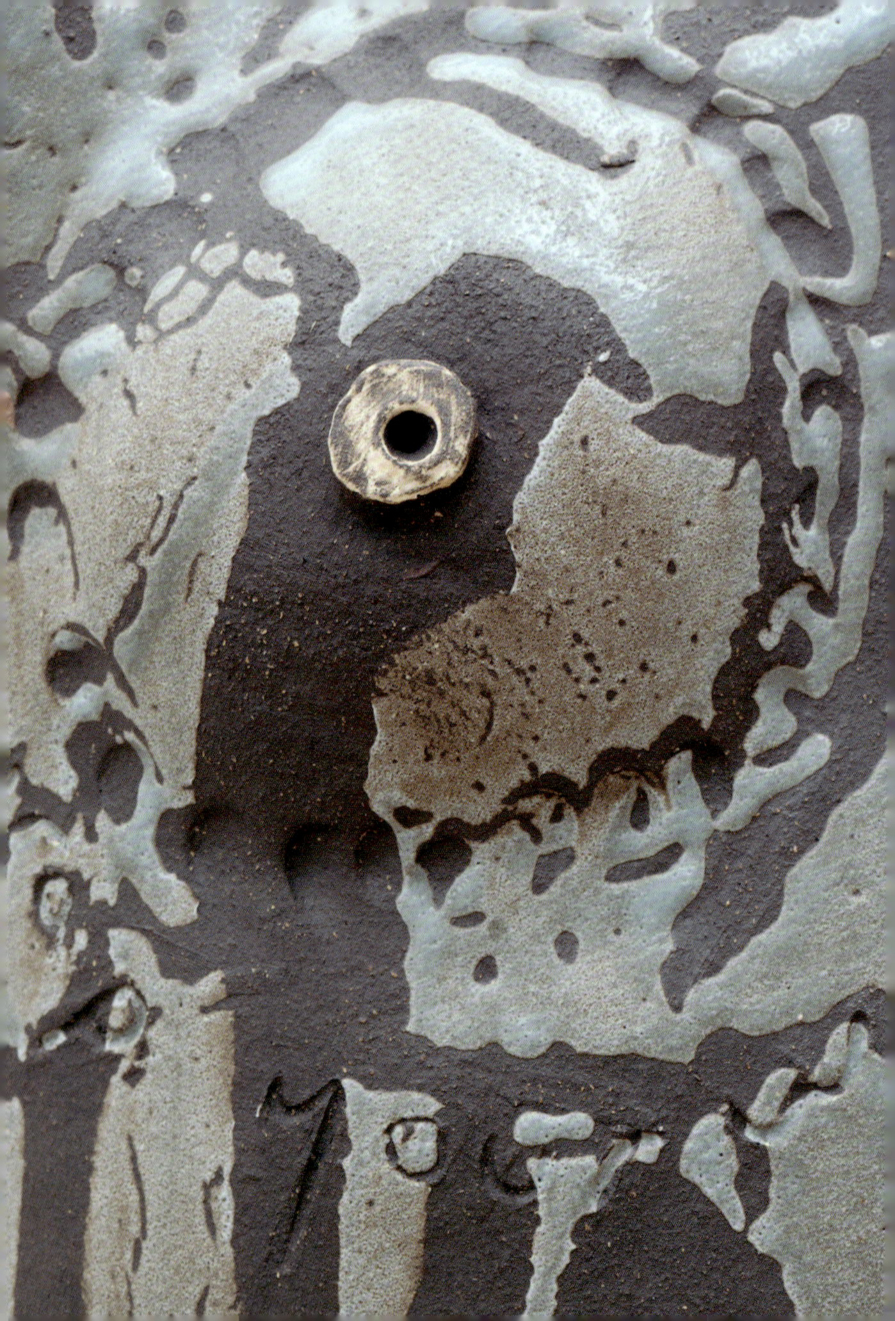

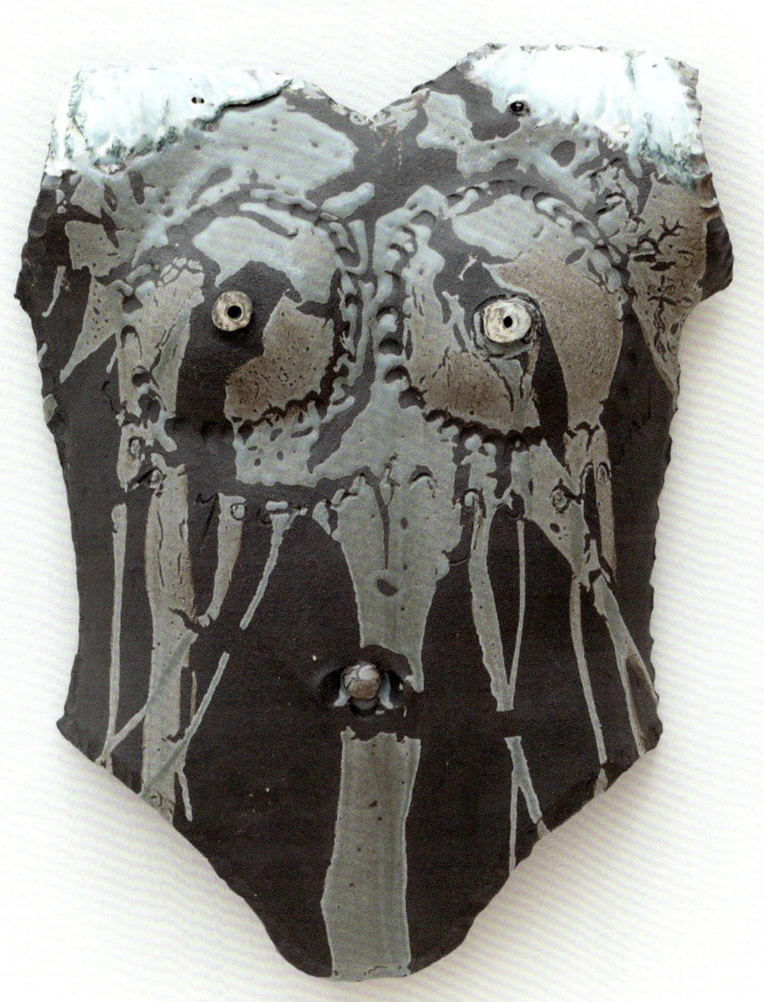

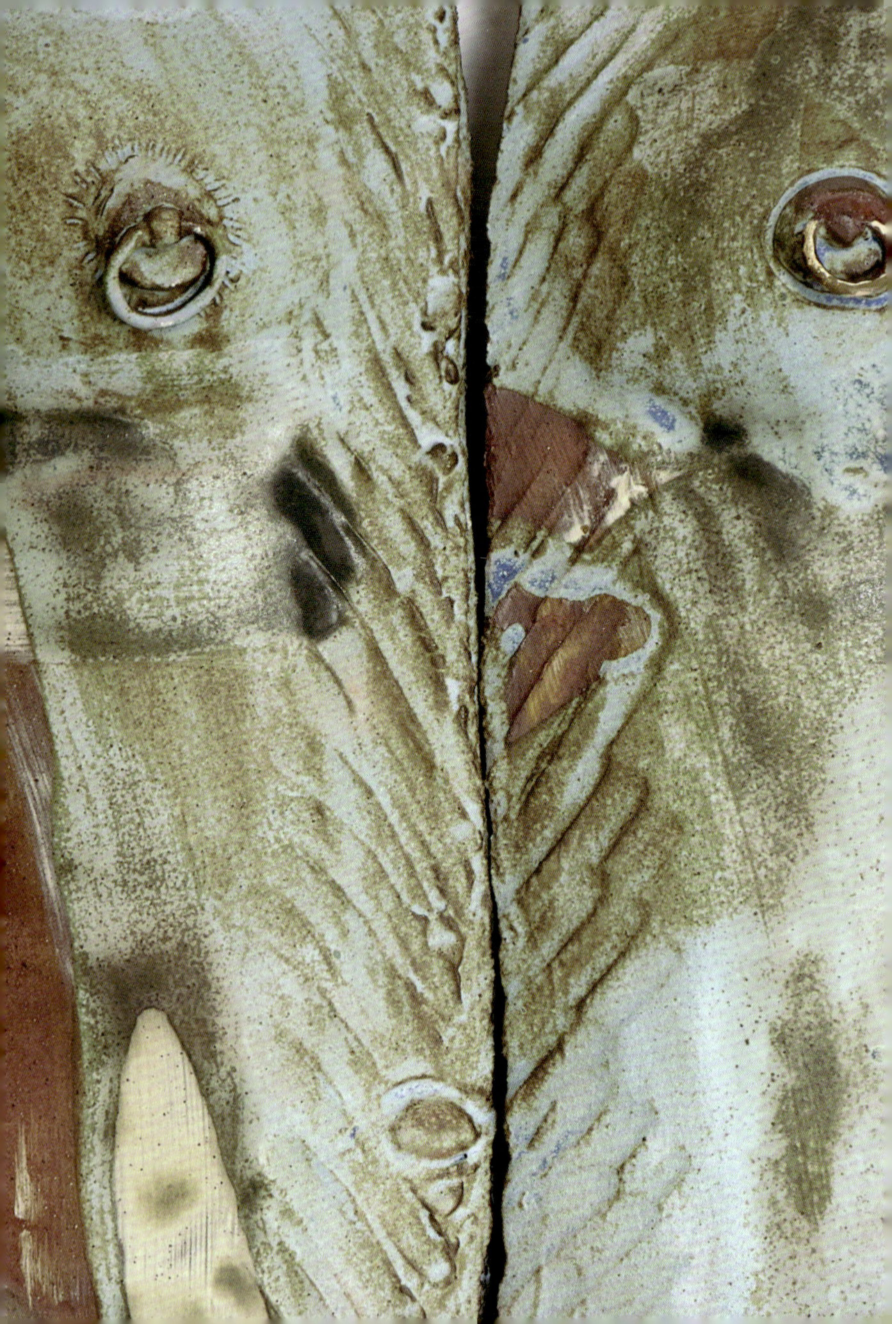

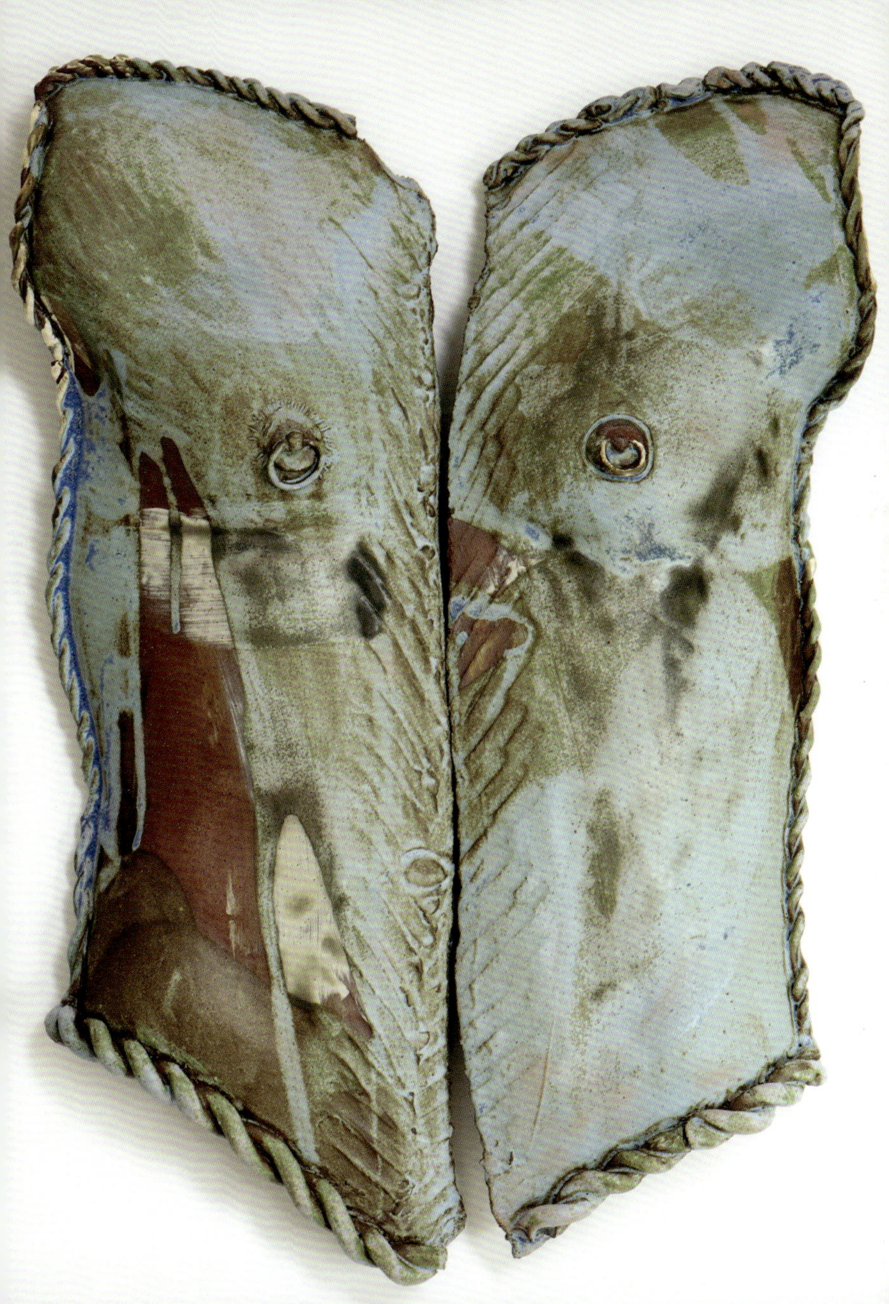

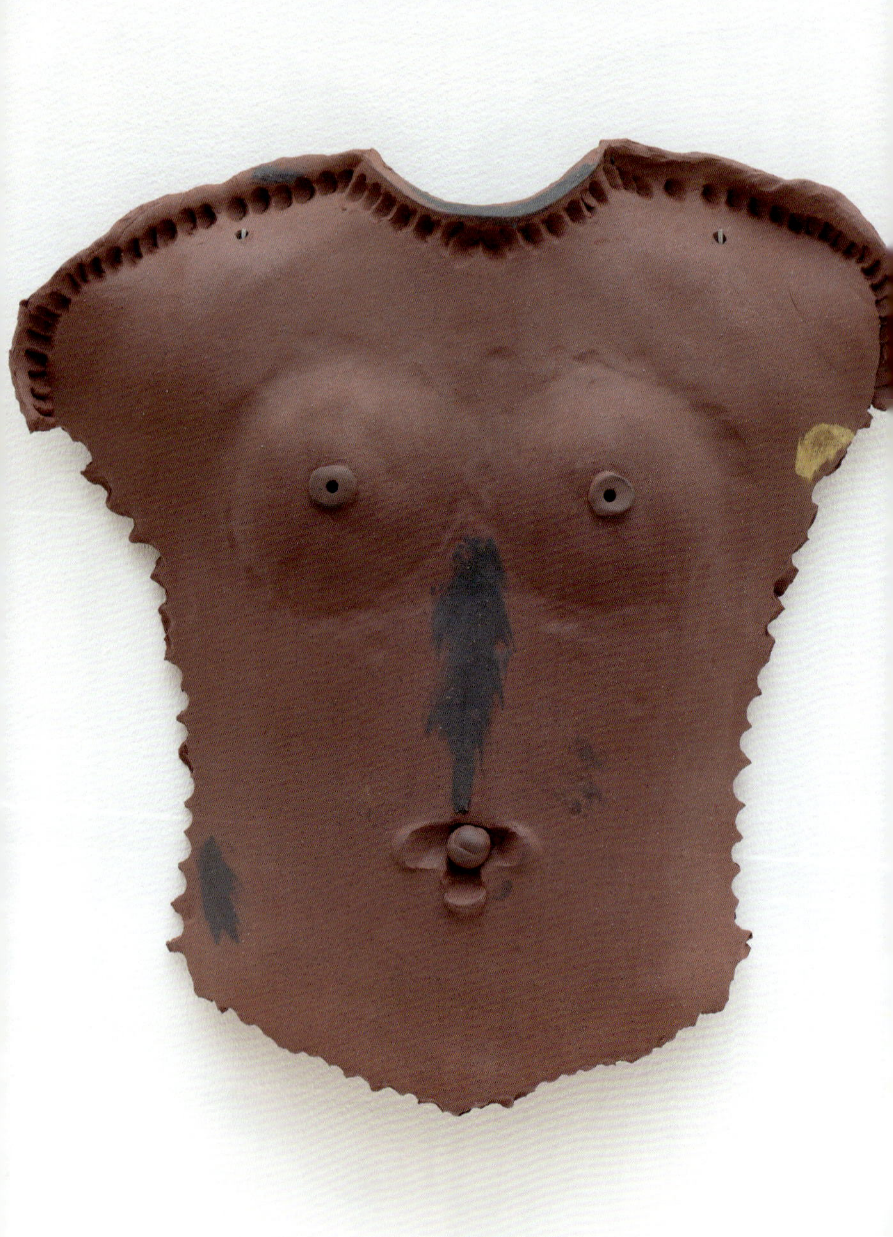

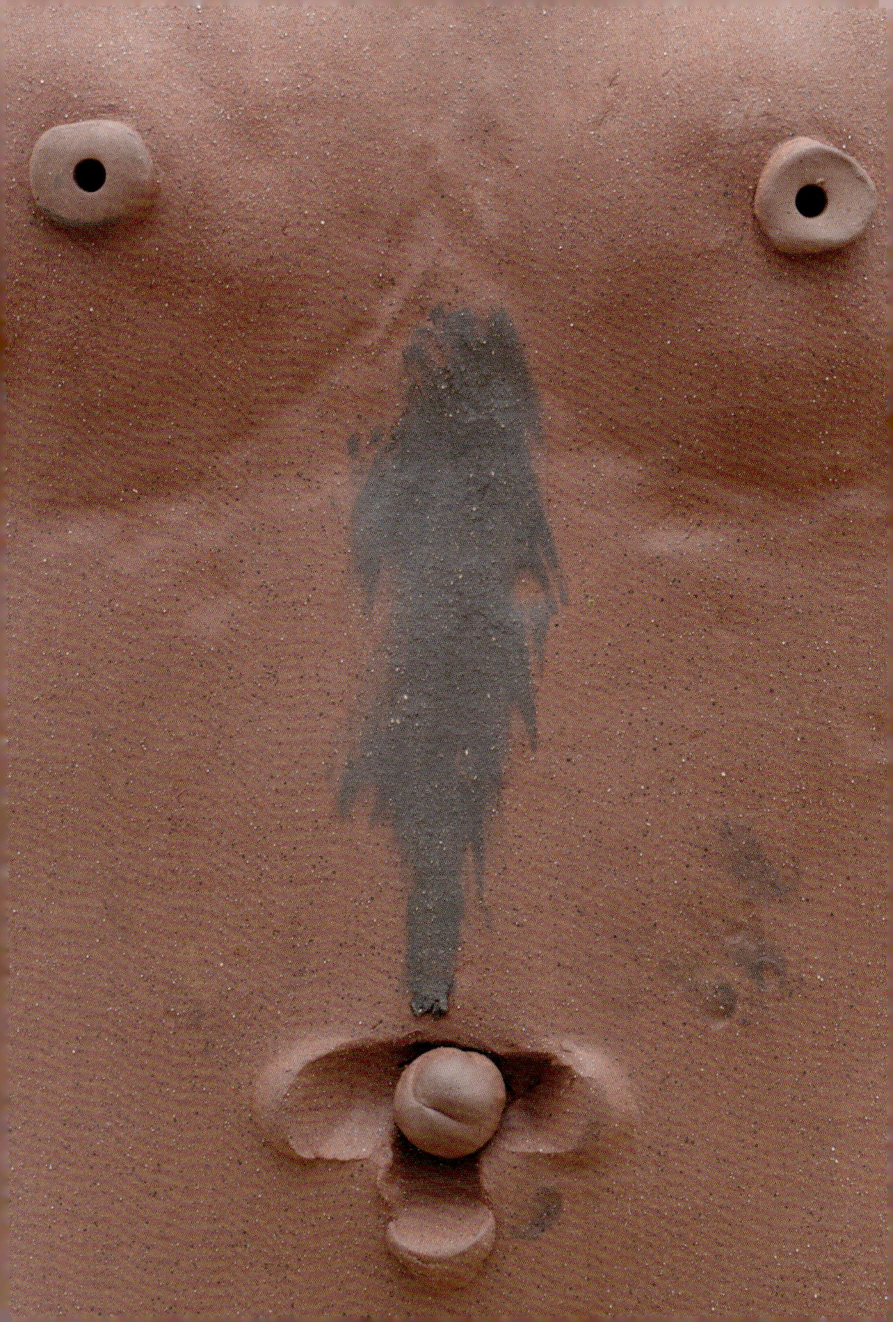

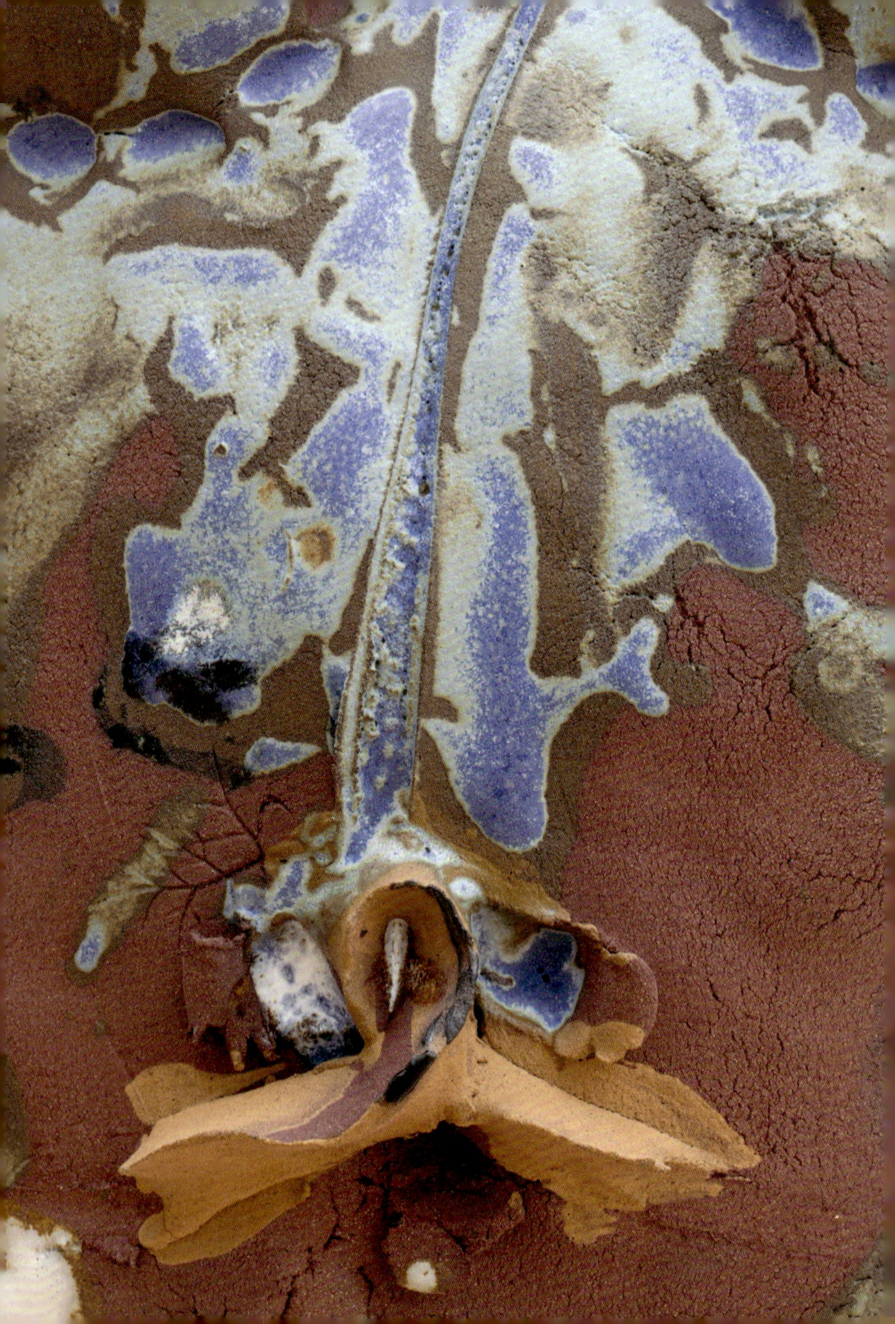

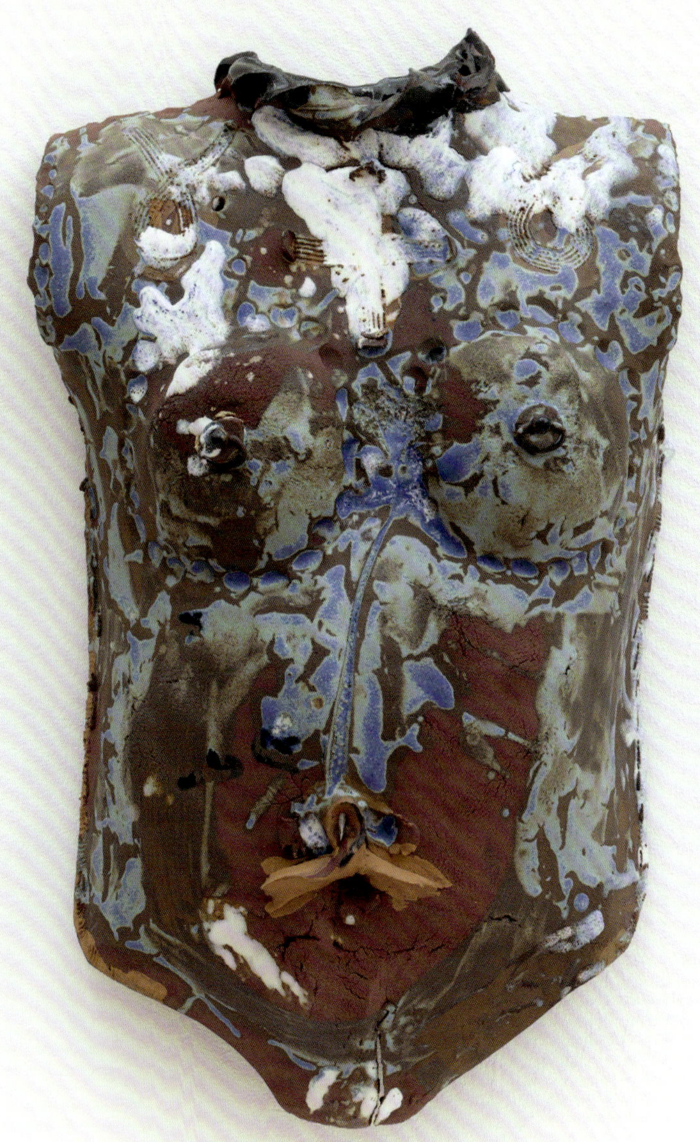

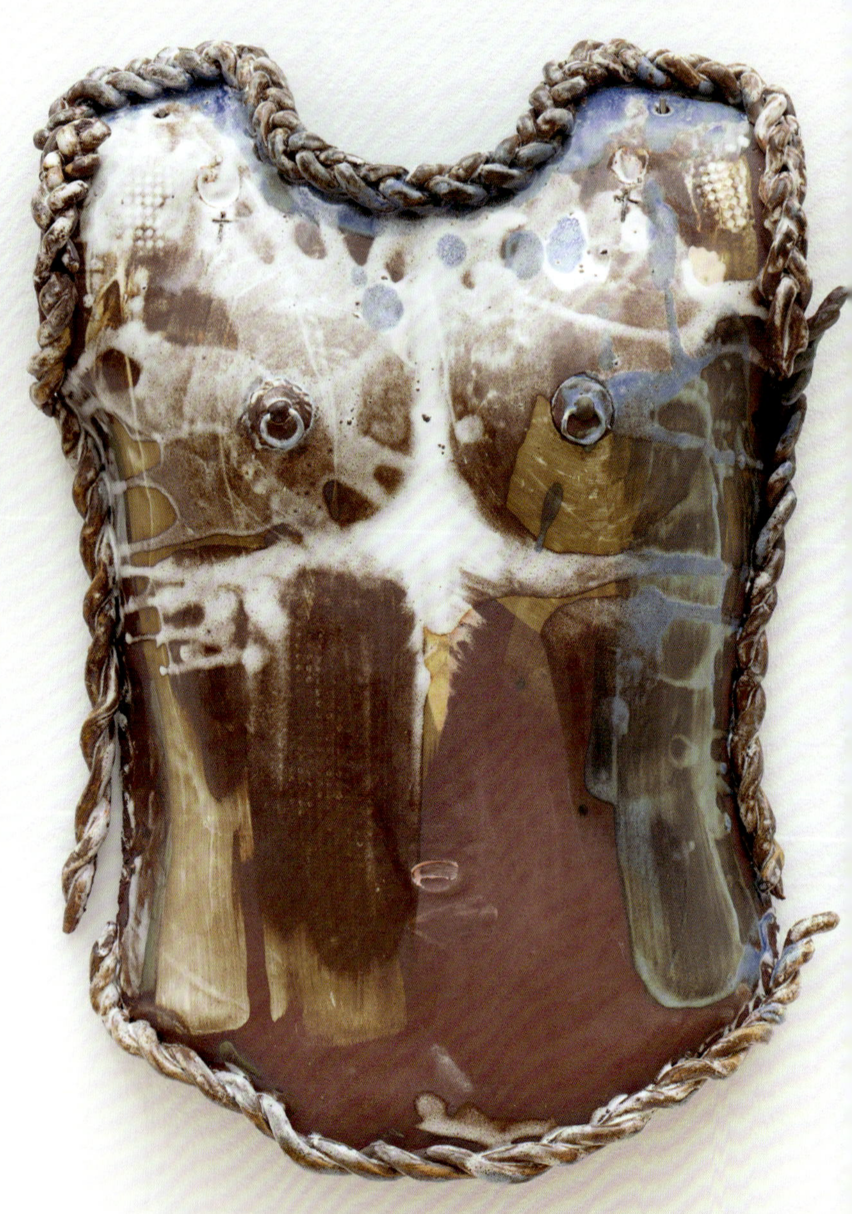

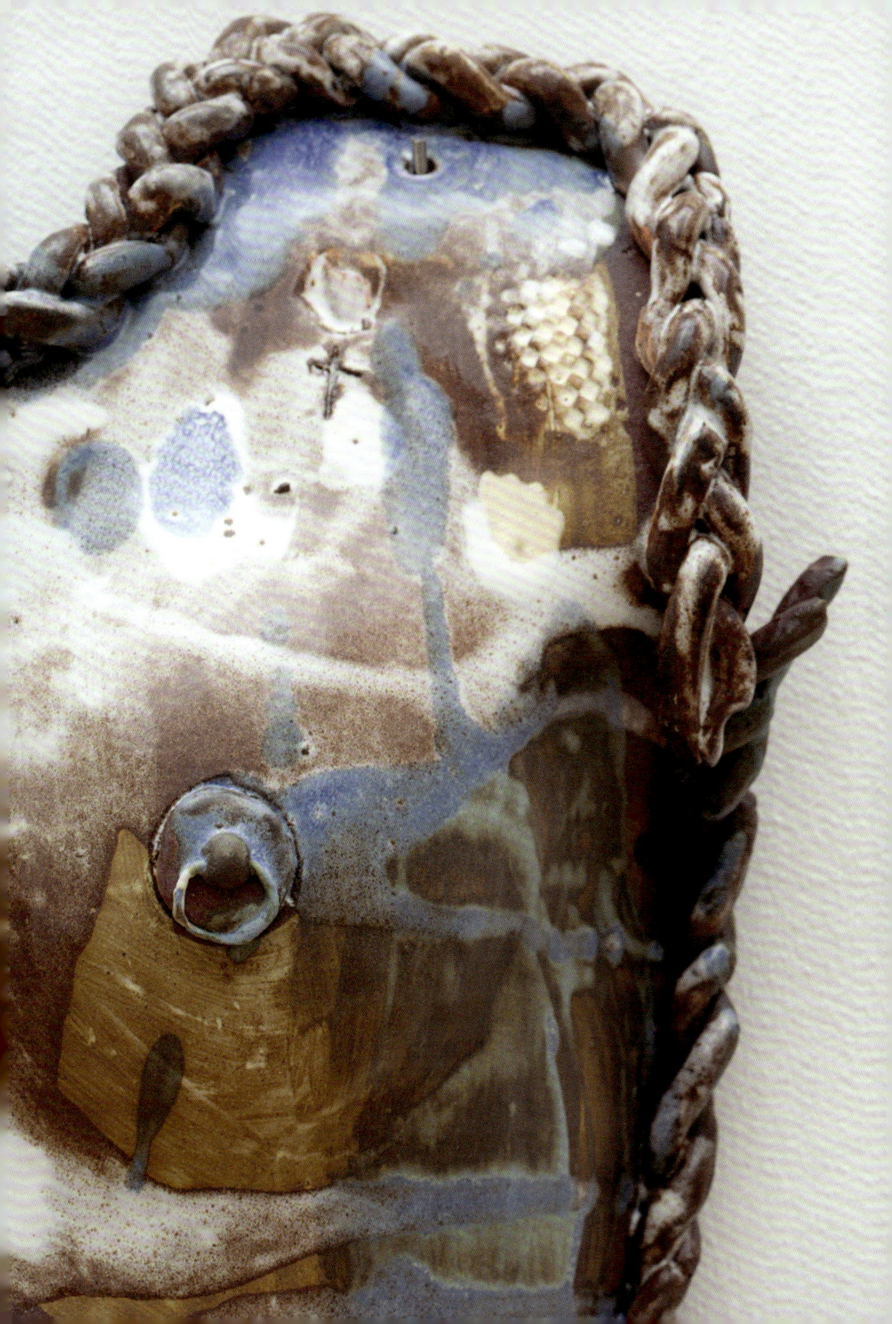

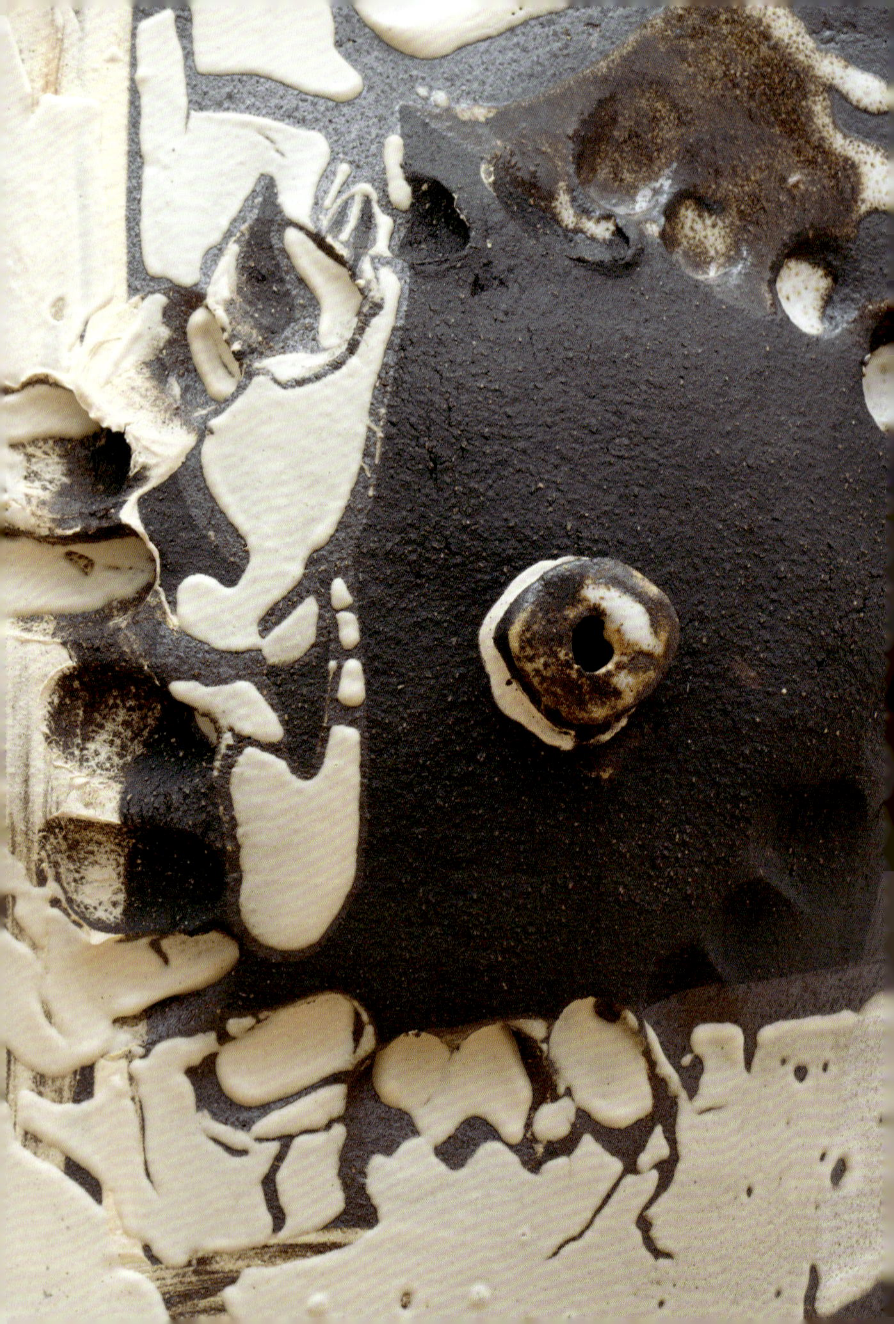

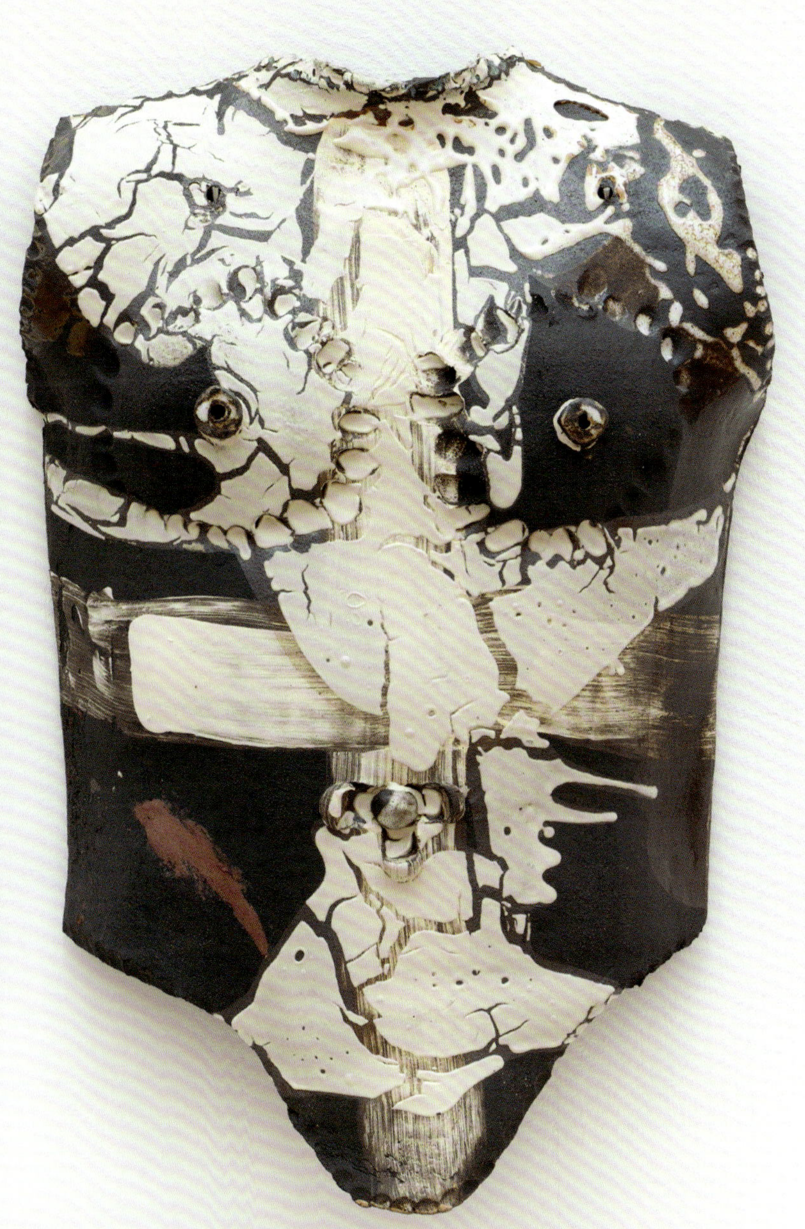

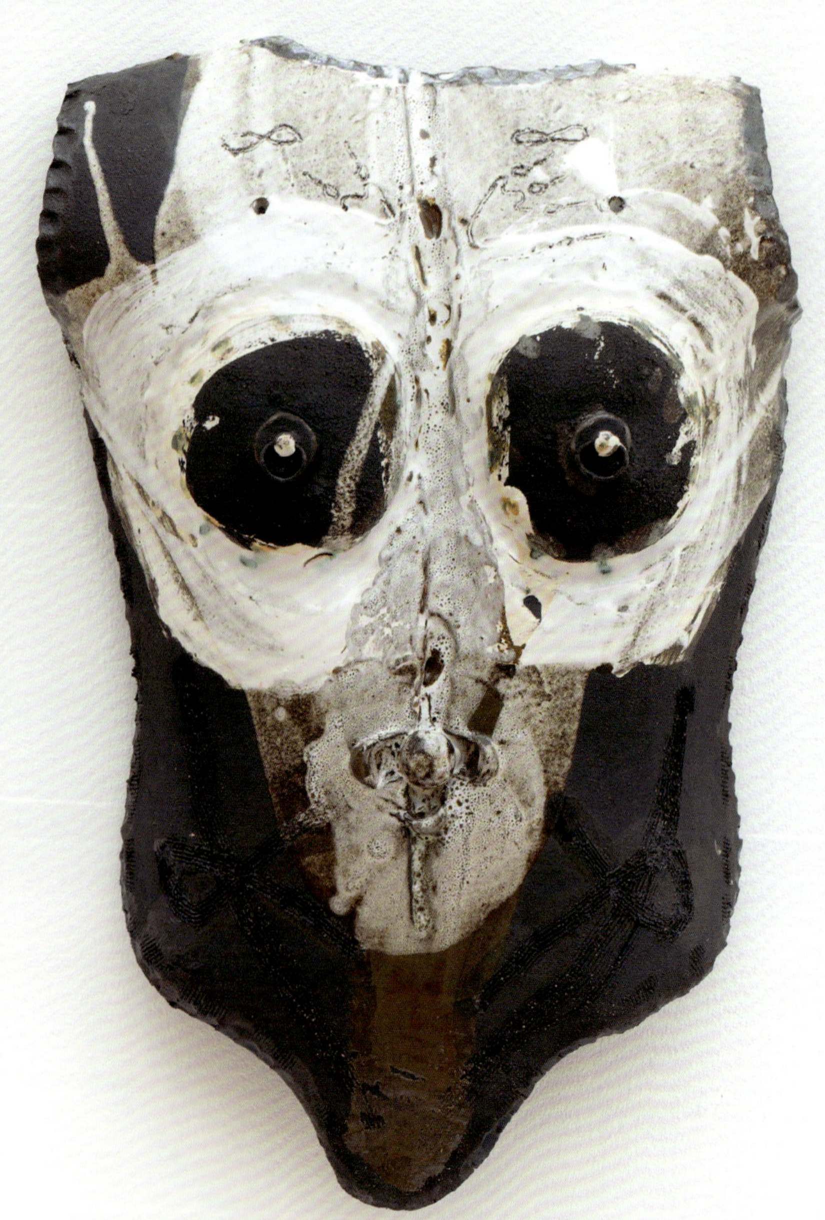

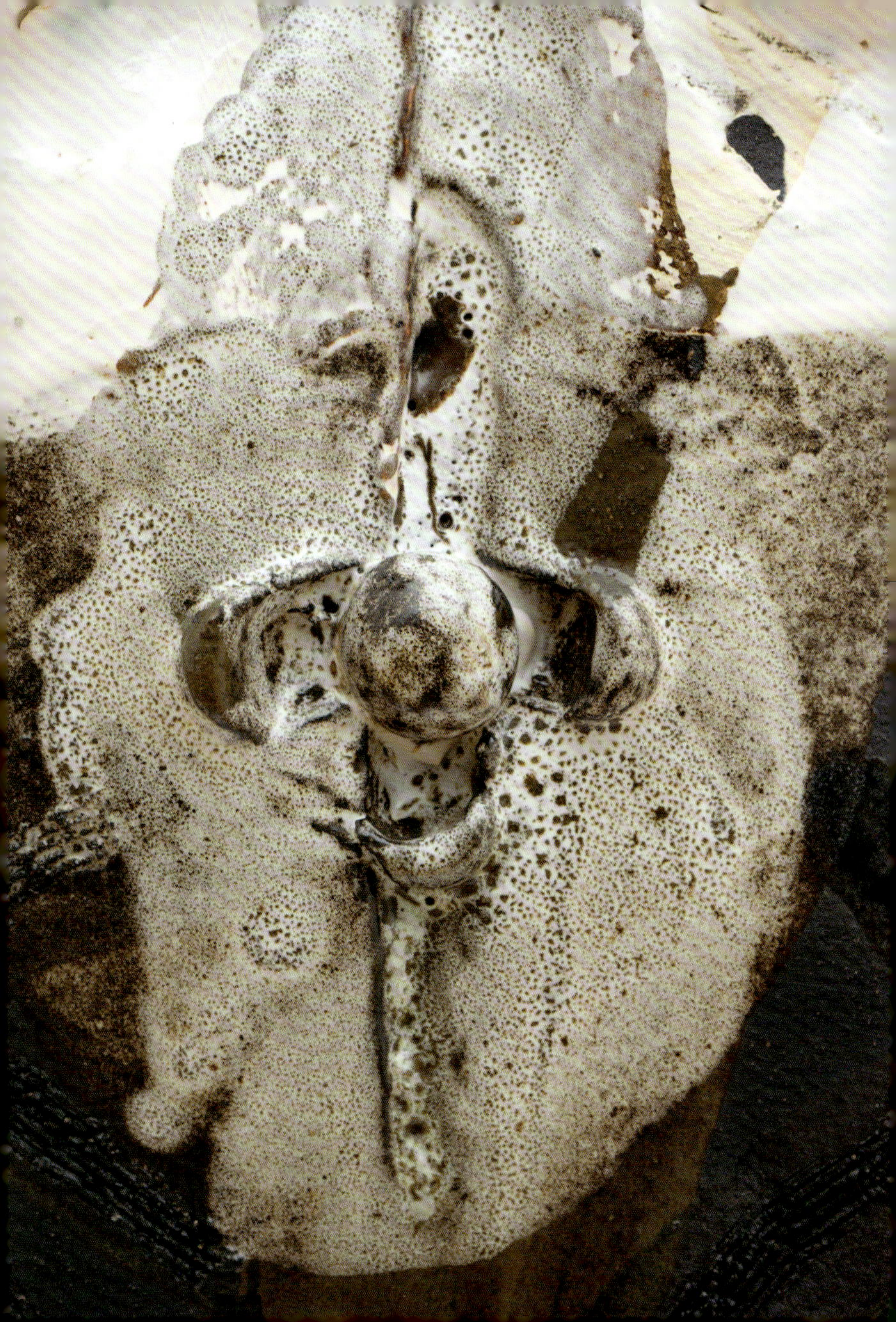

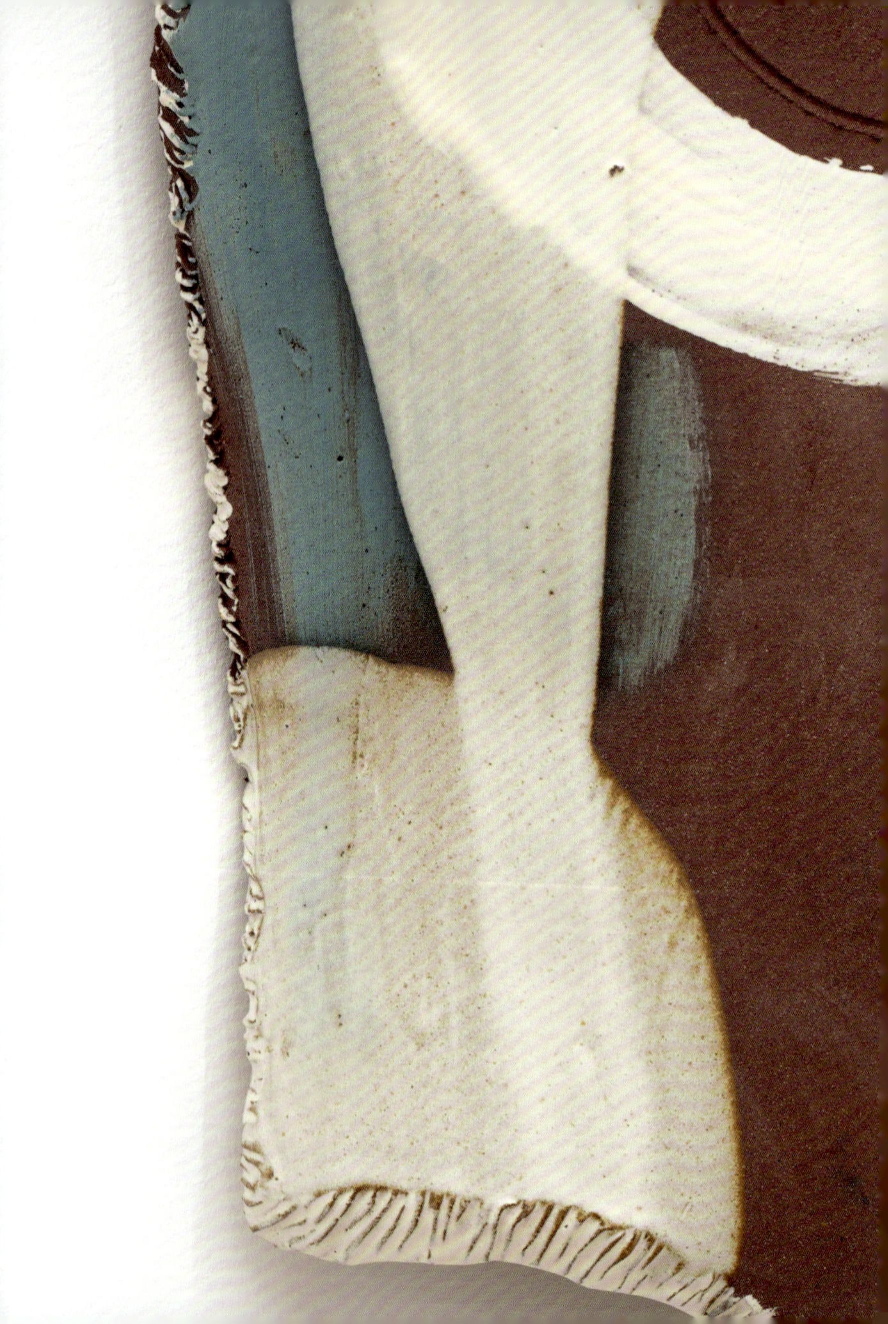

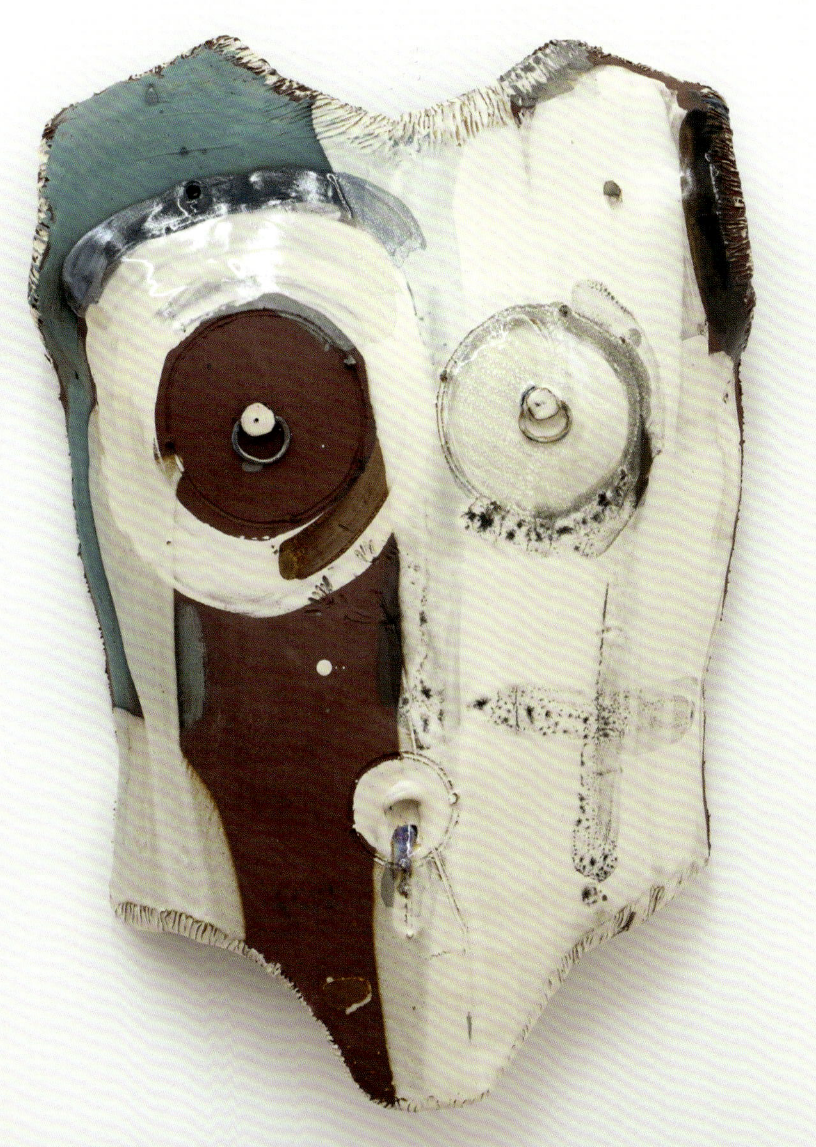

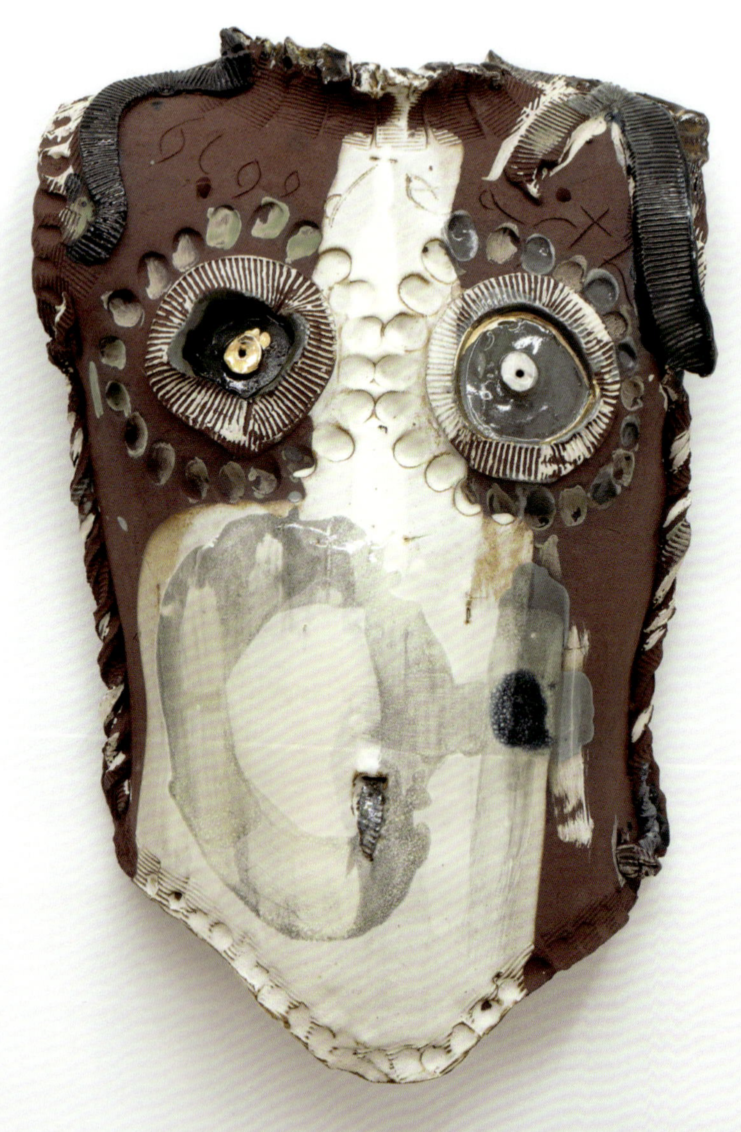

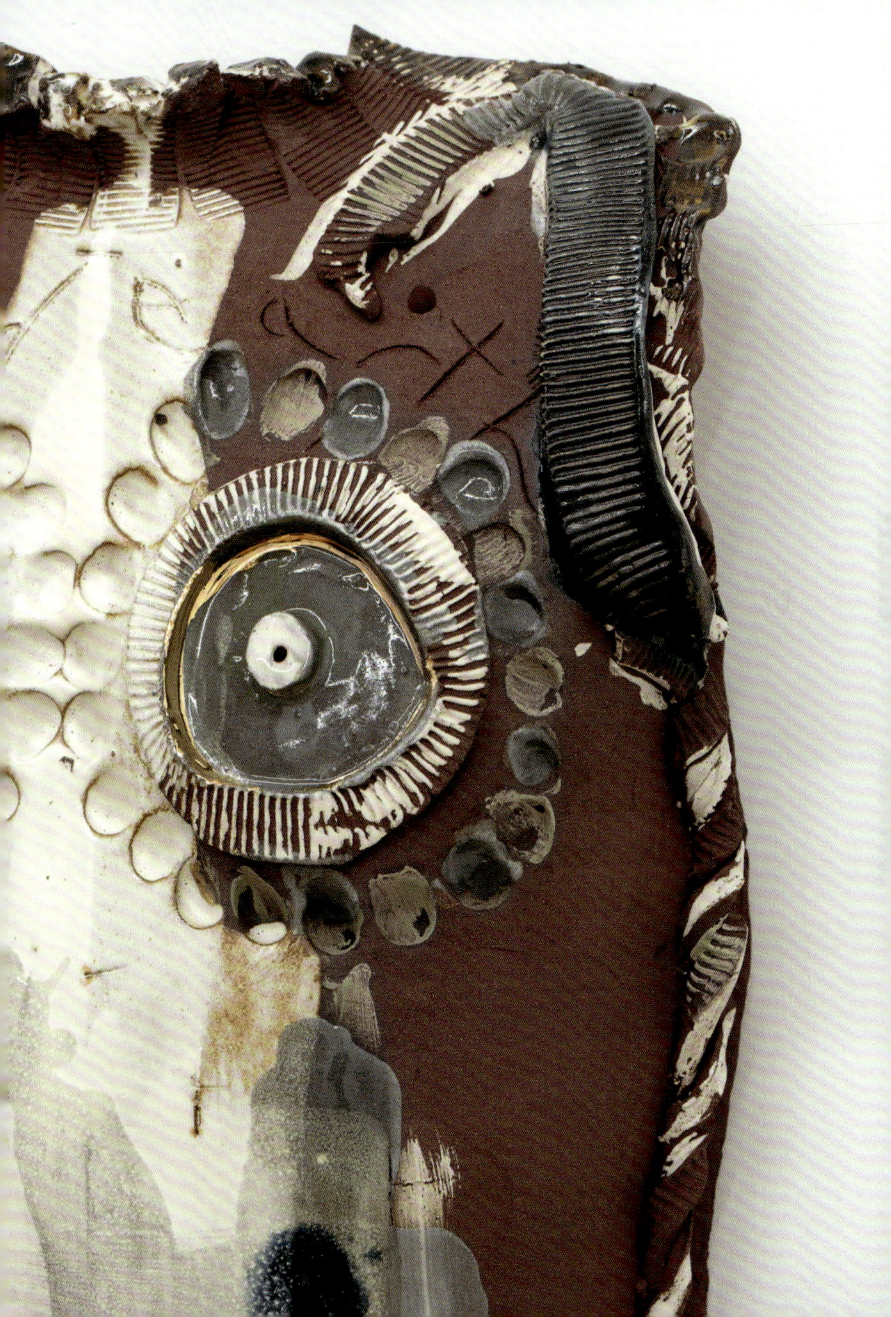

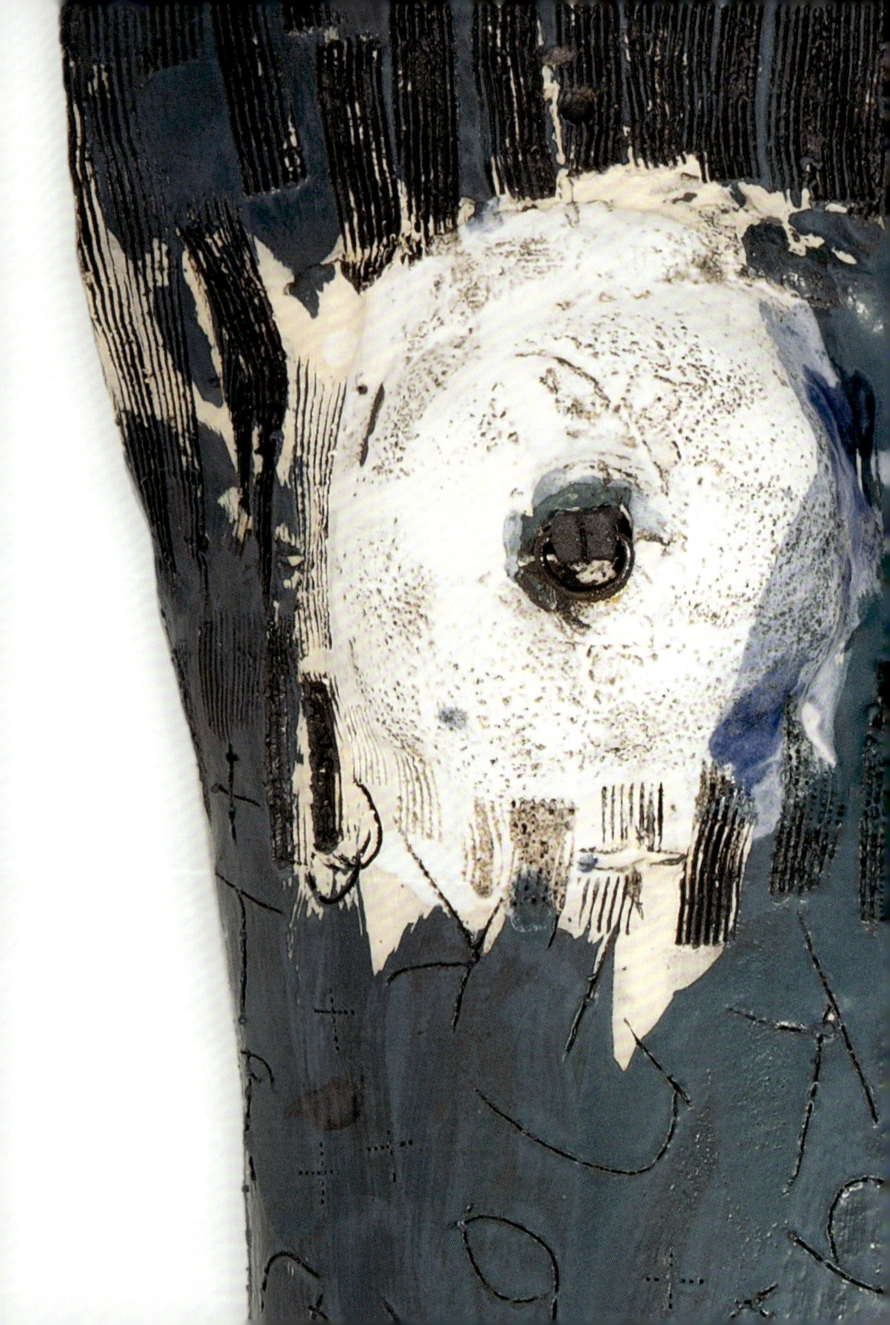

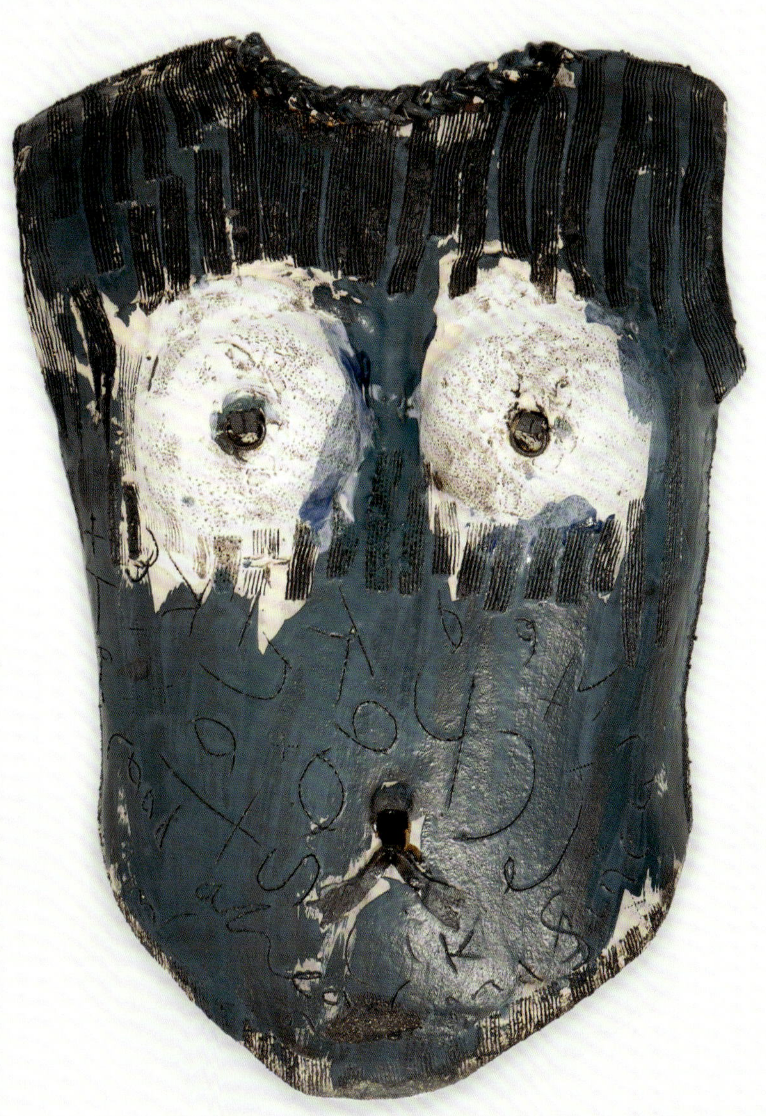

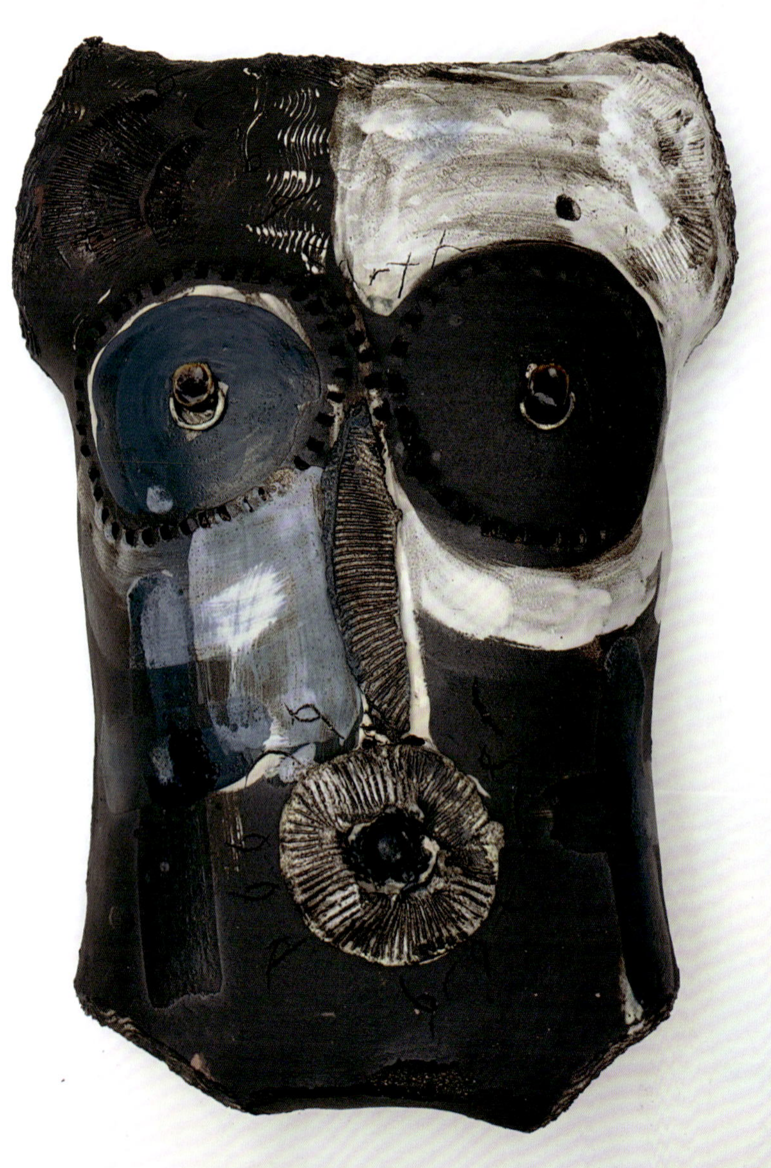

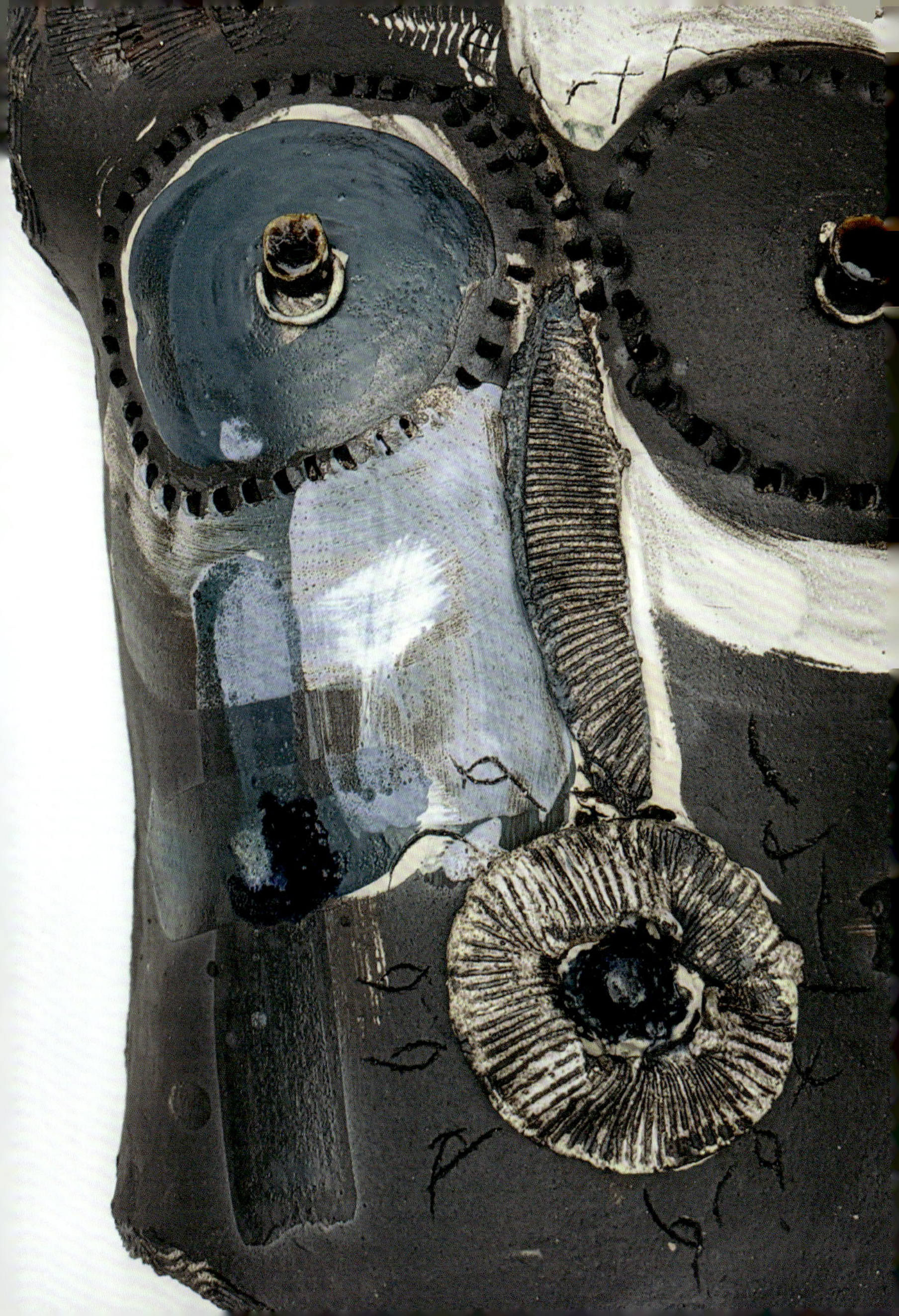

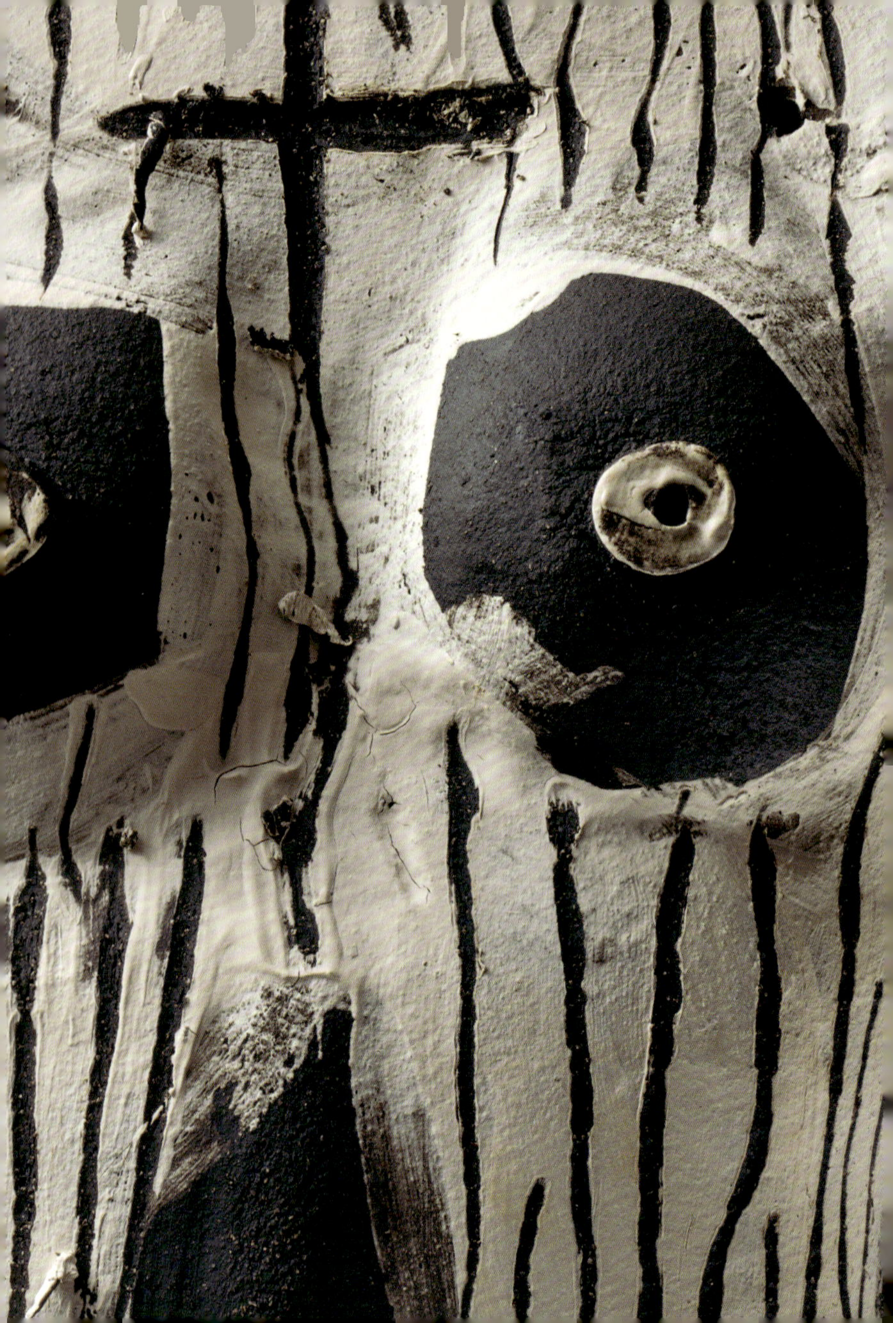

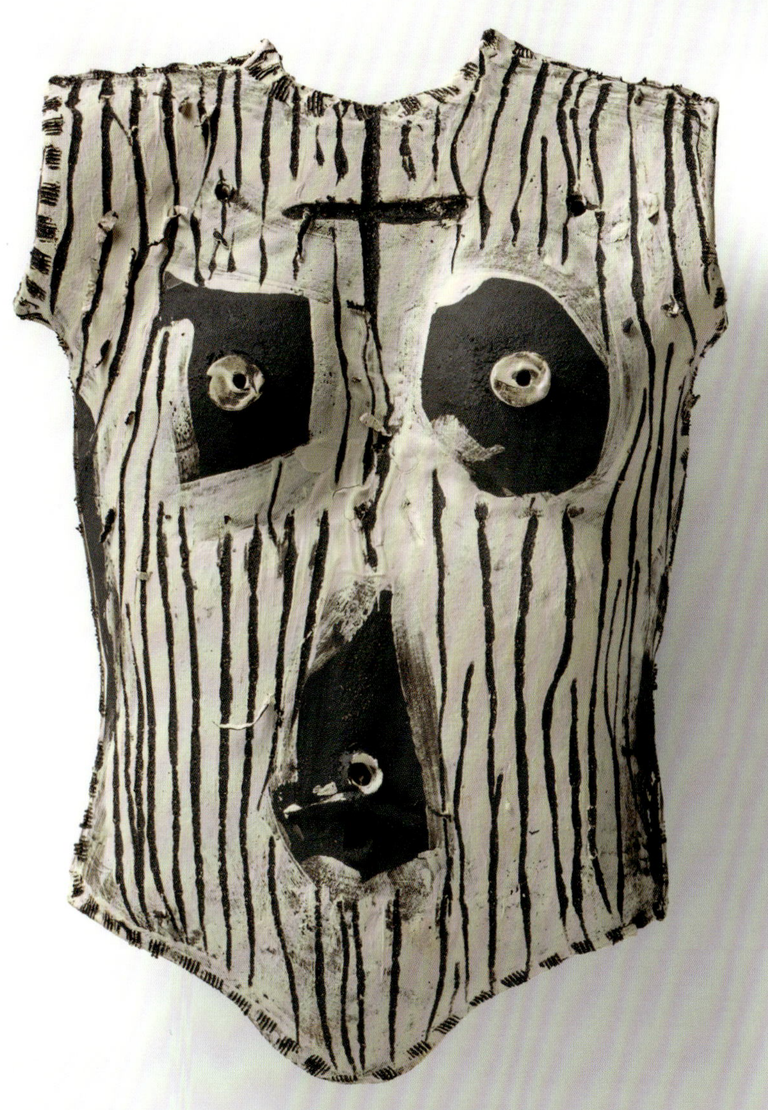

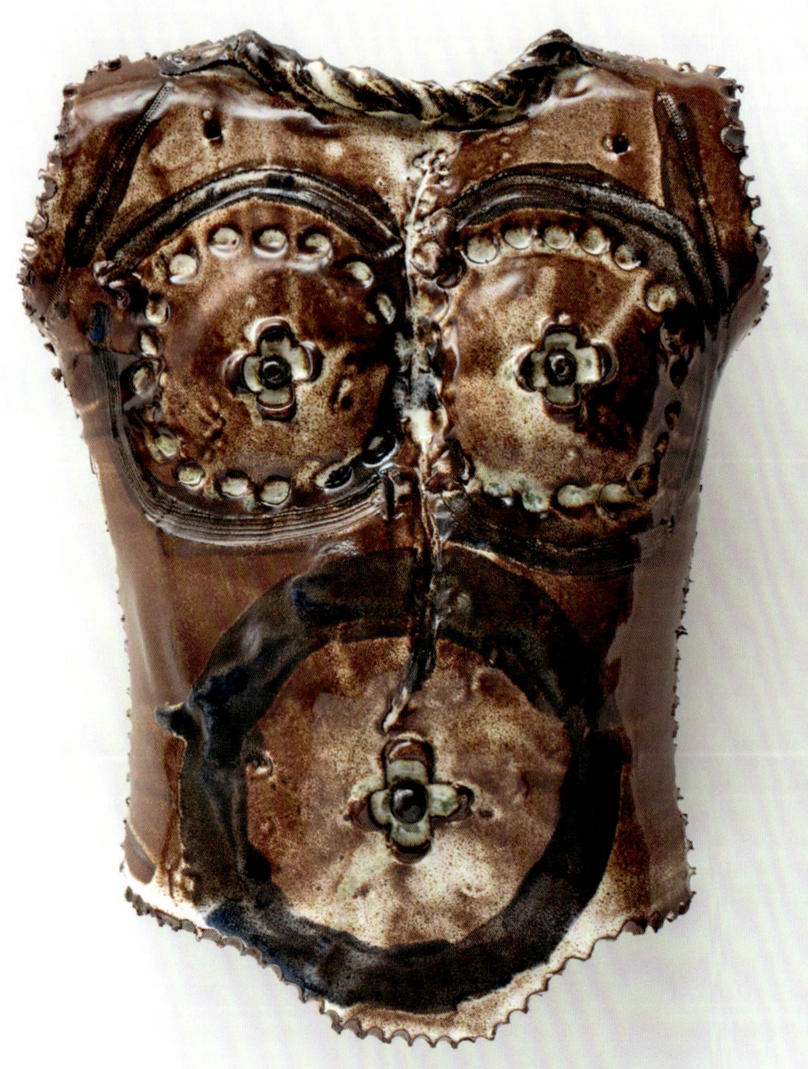

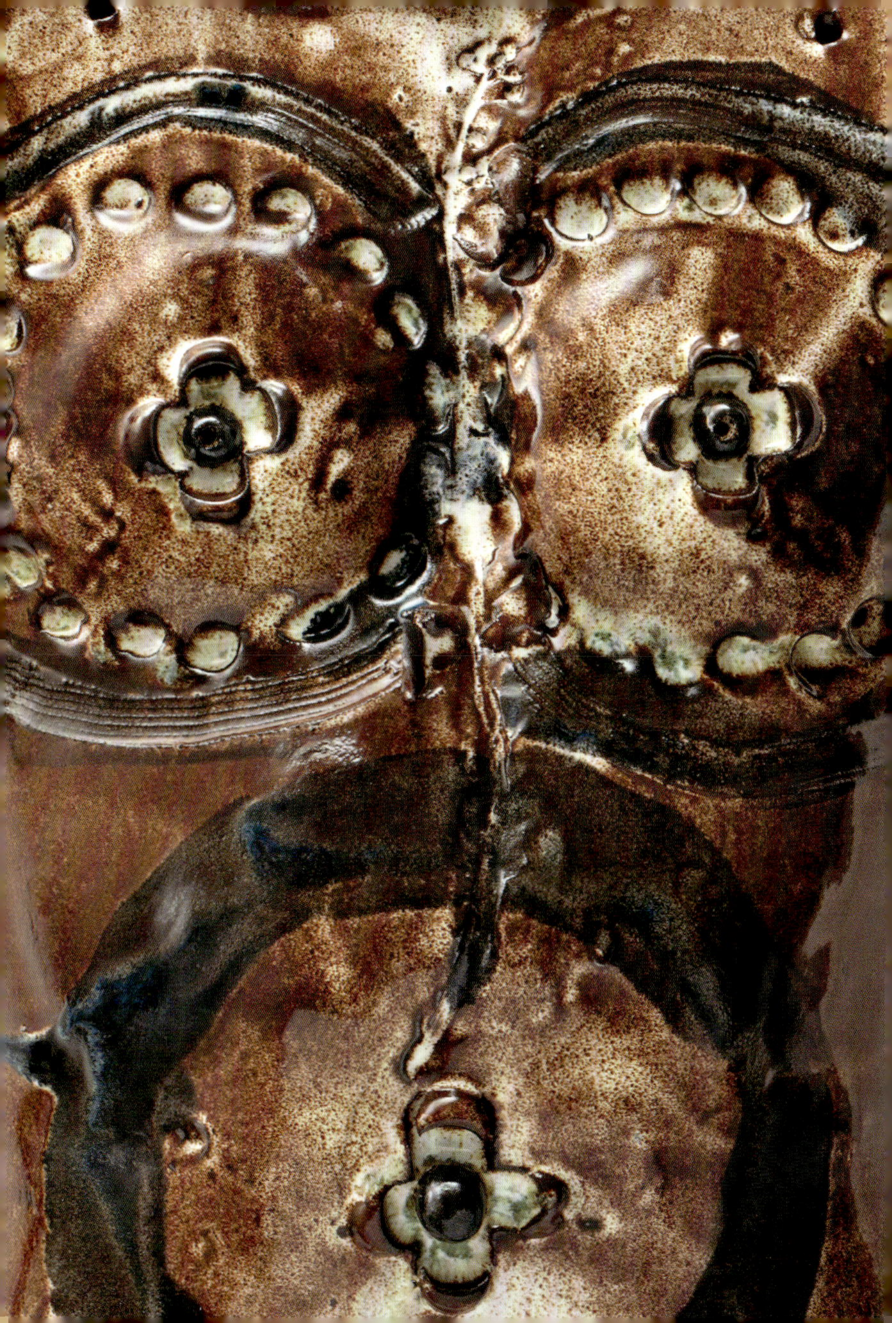

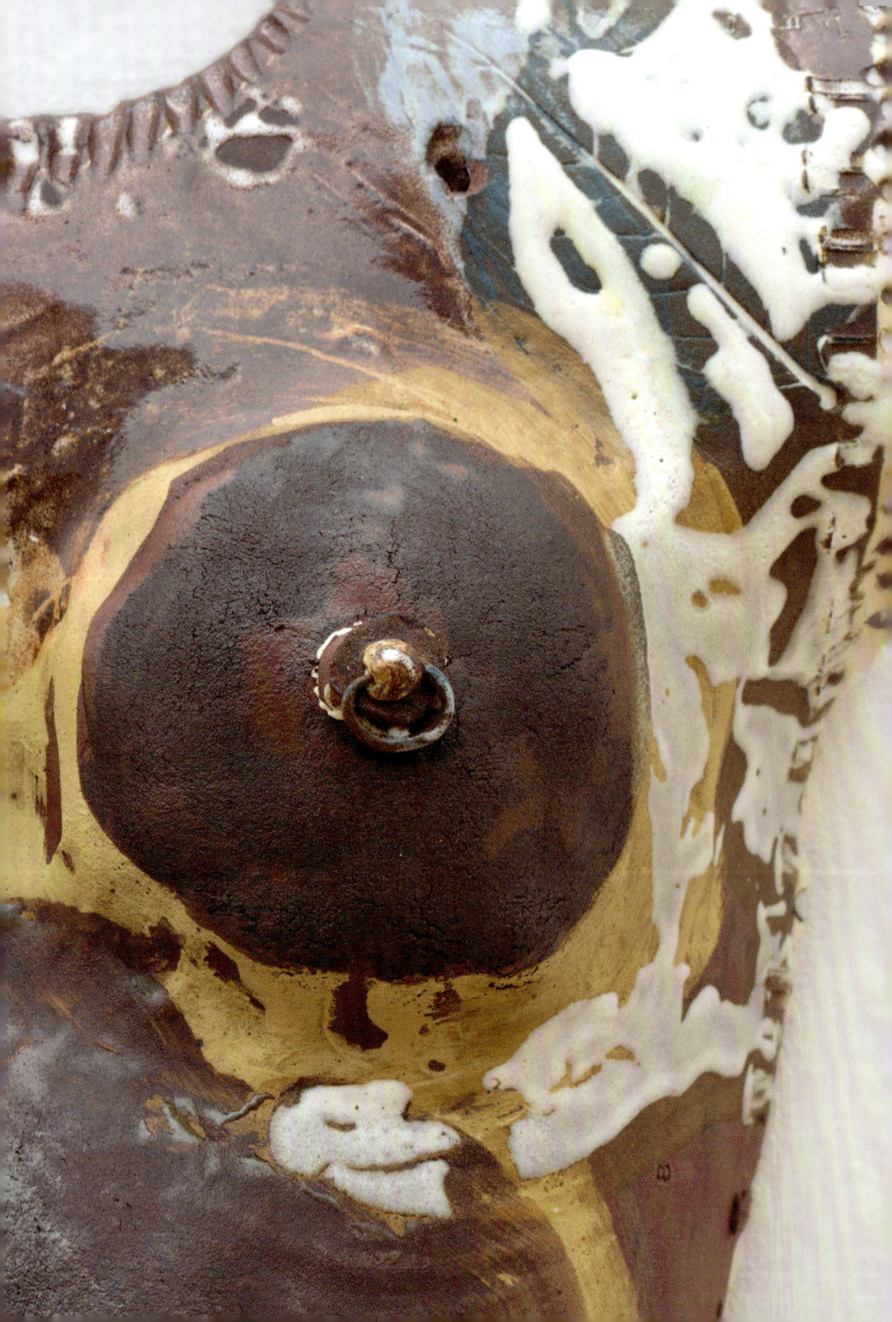

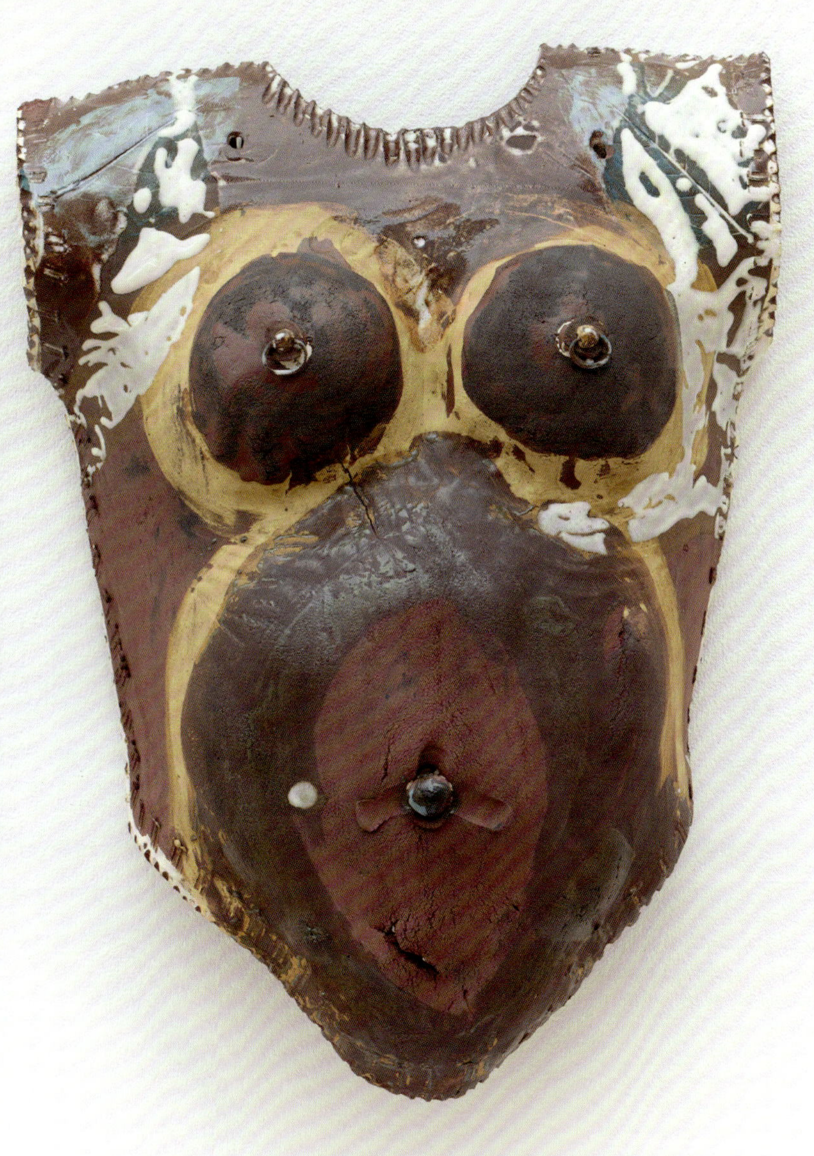

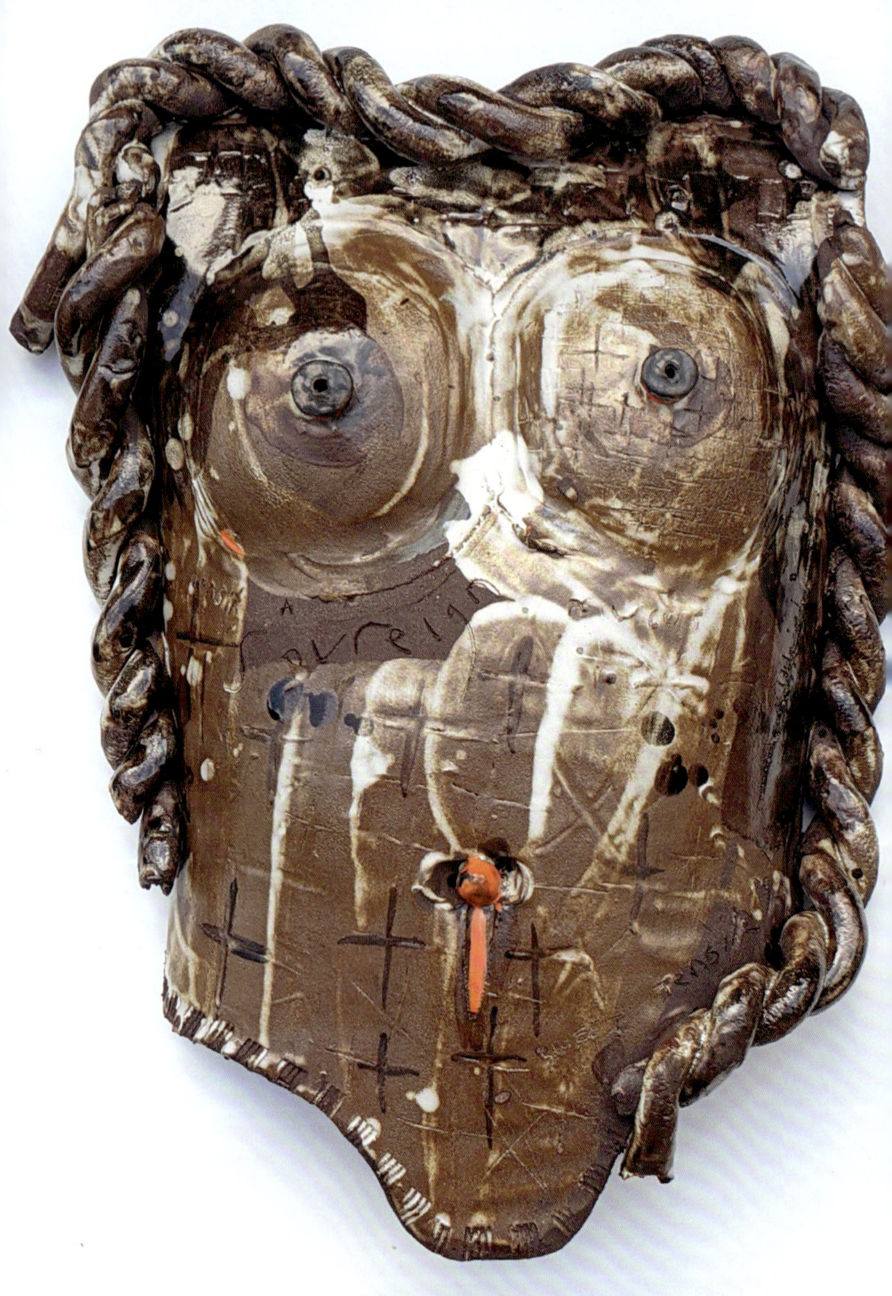

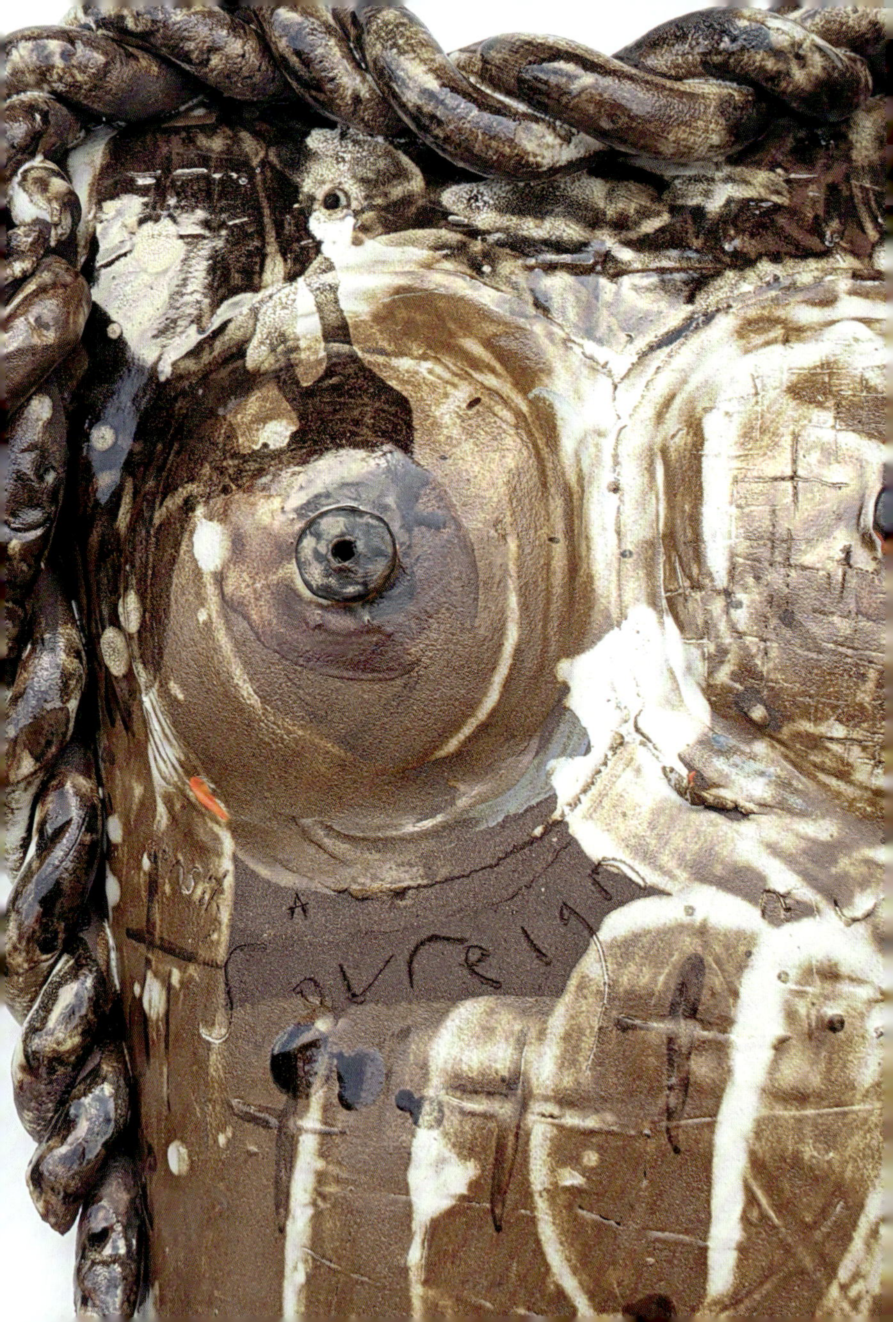
A
Sovereign

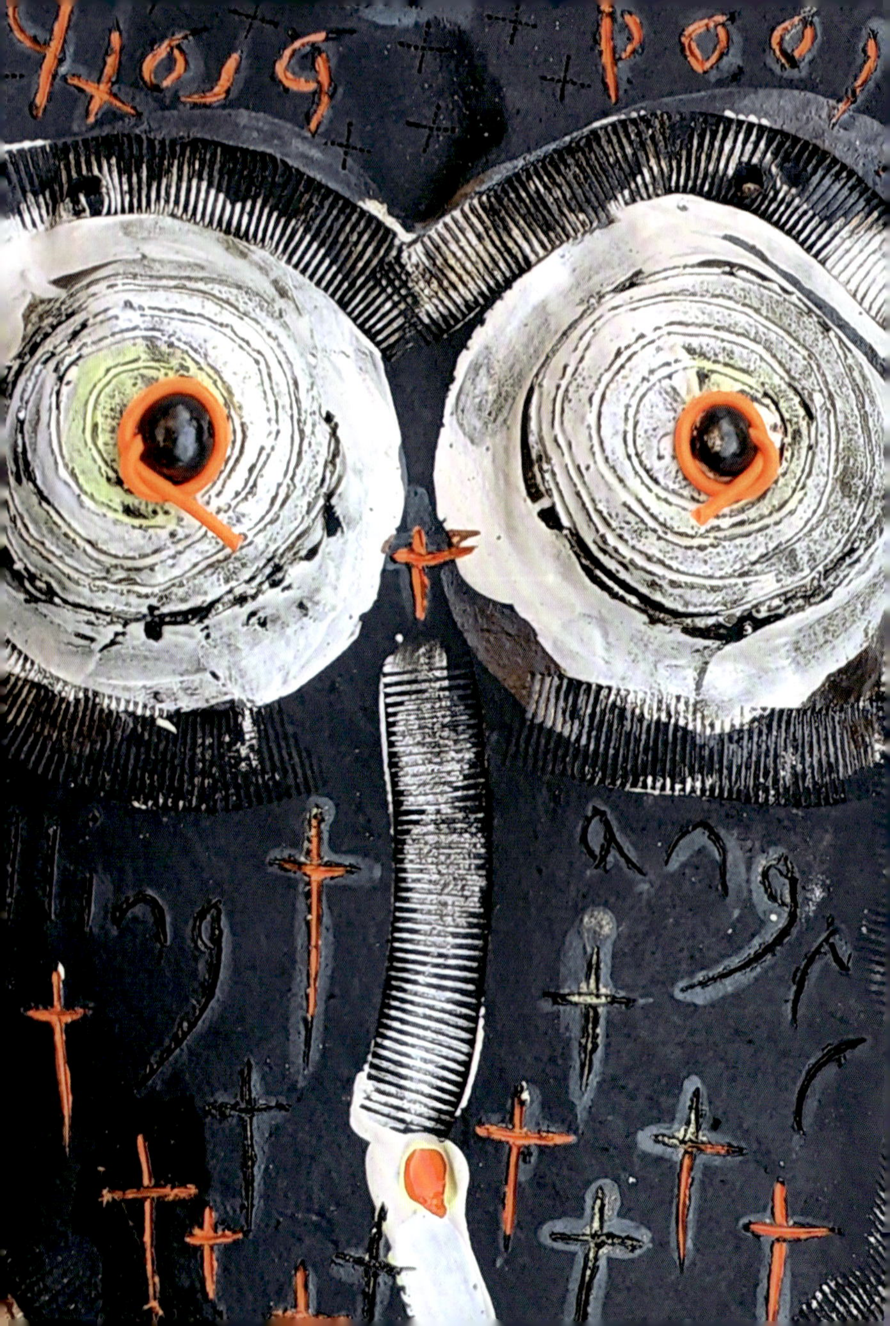

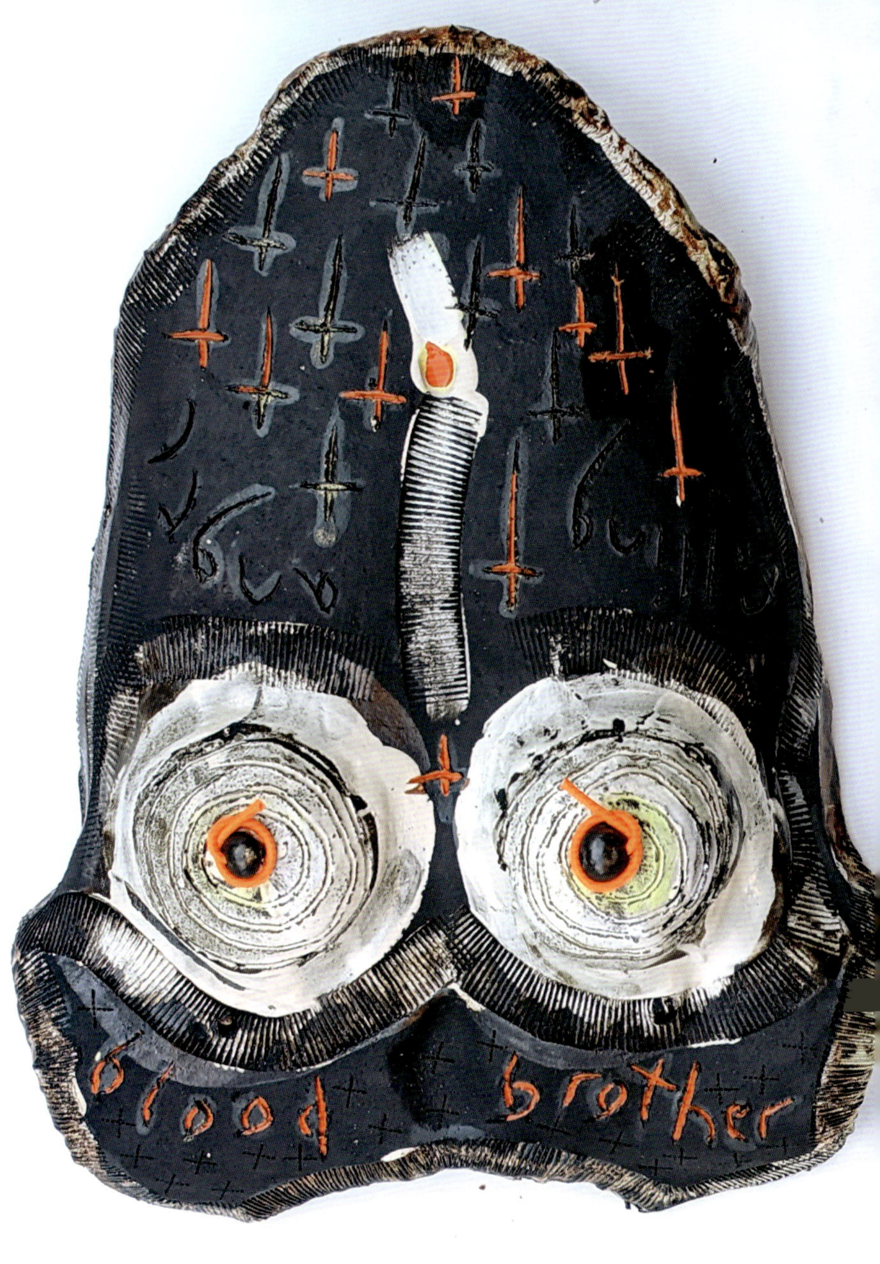

blood brother

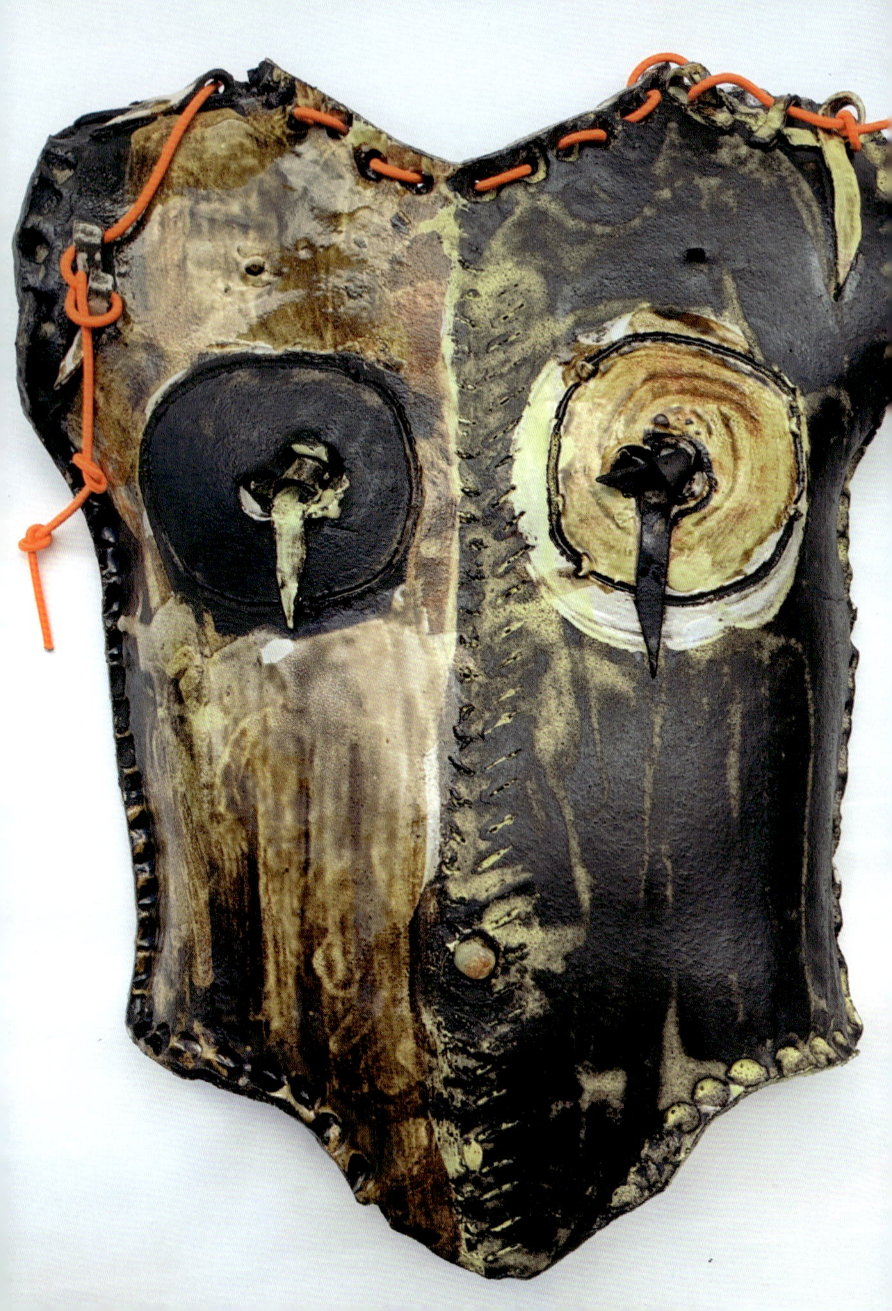

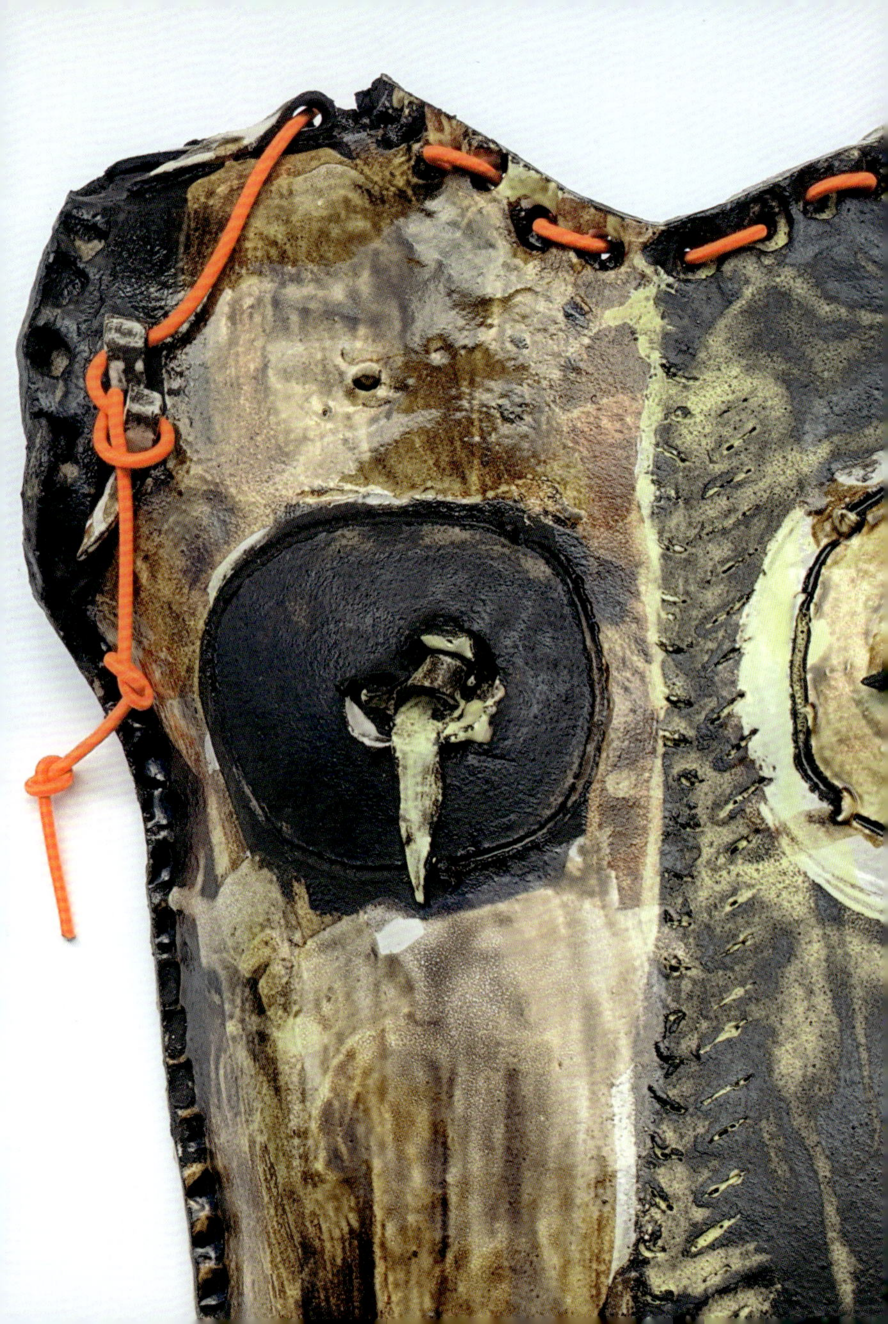

ENOUGH

SERAFINE1369

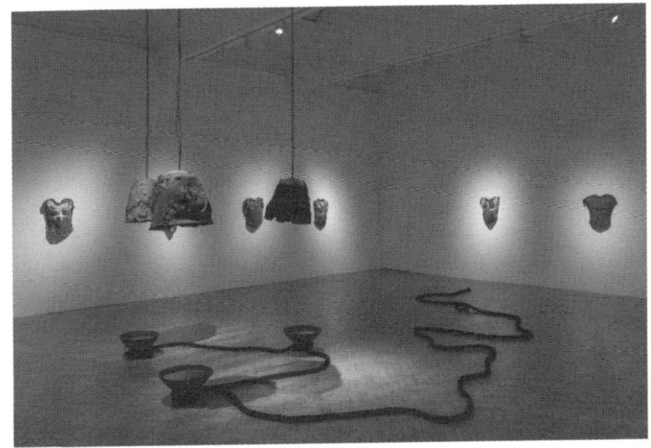

To me, Phoebe's work has always been very bodily, visceral, curious about the fleshy material that we are made of, curious to the point of violence - cracked eggs underfoot, beetroot flesh staining hands, a cow's tongue smacked onto a work surface over and over again, bodies closeup and offered like meat...Then, at some point, things that might hold and cover us entered their language - fruit nets like masks, suspension straps, vessels, armour. Always this sense of a looming threat that I might argue can come from living in a body marked by blackness.

I first saw *The subtle rules the dense* as part of the show *A Scratch! A Scratch!* at Camden Arts Centre in 2021. Baz Luhrmann's gay extravaganza *Romeo + Juliet* made a mark on both of us (Phoebe and I) as teenagers, a slick and gaudy celebration of the tragedy of falling in love. Or something. All very angsty. Hopeless kids, useless adults inviting them into a system only set up for endless war. Heart overriding head in the name of rational logic. Belief systems that will only betray you, the material stuff of you, the skin, flesh, bloody fact of you.

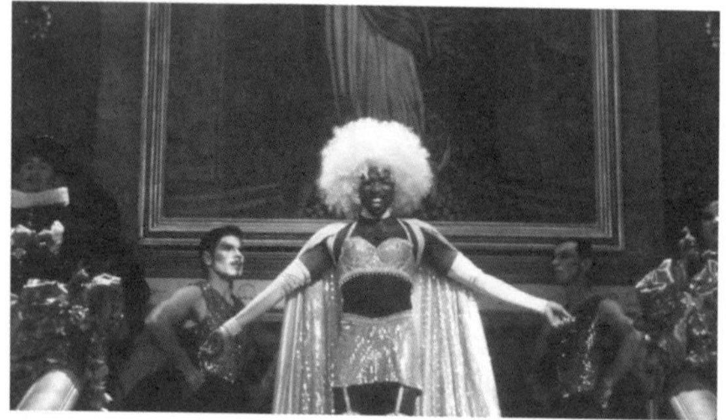

Still from *Romeo + Juliet* (1996). Centre: Mercutio (Harold Perrineau)

Mercutio, the character who is quoted in the show title, played by Harold Perrineau, opens the portal into other worlds and dies a bloody, messy death in this one, as he holds tight to the rules of a game that can only betray him. The character carries the burden of being the queer trickster - because queers are all too often represented as magical, tragic, tricksters, bodies vulnerable to penetration and spirits dissolving the illusory boundaries between worlds - a messenger, a prophet, whose life is lived to make things visible for those who could not see. An intersectional meeting place perceived to be at the margins, on the periphery, complicated and not quite graspable but neces- sary for defining a sense of comfortable centre. Mercutio's action is the thing at the edge which impacts the entire narrative, he is only doing what has been asked and yet he becomes a symbol of the dysfunction and shame of society, a motivator for what follows. Fragile permeable body. Mercutio is magical and vibrant and demanding to be met with gusto by the world and all of that prowess disappears with a scratch.

Absent a head, the chest plates in *The subtle rules the dense* call forth the energy and importance of the torso, housing the heart, the lungs, the stomach, the centre of us.

There are no eyes here, no mouth, but the entire machinery
of our organs and the tenderness of the skin, flesh and
armour of muscle that protect them. Baring one's chest
can be both a declaration of battle, and an expression of
intimate vulnerability. Here is what is at stake, what your gut
knows, not what your eyes might tell you; the chest is blind.

We talk about 'mental health' when the declarations of
knowledge from our different organs - each with their own
kinds of 'sight' - do not match up with one another, nor with
the narrative we should follow in order to move forward
smoothly in society. I see in these chest plates a desire to
protect the heart and guts over the head. Love and rage.
Protecting and declaring the love and fire in the heart, the
rage and instinct in the gut. Dealing with invisible things,
things that others cannot see, is a conversation between
genius and insanity. If the person navigating invisible words,
threats, messages, is black then the pendulum of judgement swings towards the latter.

A mask is never the full story but a tool, a shield, a signifier.
Masks can be about protection, and also interruption, an
intervention in the flow of things, a re-routing, redirecting of
understanding and the terms of engagement in relationship.
This can be a defence strategy, a form of protection or
conscious attempt at transformation. As a kid, I was afraid
of masks, confused by the barrier, the redirection, the
stillness of them. Particularly when they were not being
worn and were just sitting there, or hanging on walls, faces
without bodies, frozen in a single expression, repeating the
same thing over and over. There's a madness in the stillness
and repetition that I would find haunting. Something unre-
solved, always ready, always there to remind you.

A friend of mine had a residency at a museum, he was
thinking about artefacts, tools, stolen from Africa and
held there, categorised as charms. Or as other things.
The violence of categorisation is that if you follow it, you
are operating on a misrepresentation from the start. I
think about all these objects, 'primitive bowl', 'ceremonial
bracelet', 'ritual stick', put on display, harmless, silent,
ancient objects. But no object is silent, right, being made
of the same materials as everything on this earth; we are
caught in inescapable, continuous conversation, held
together by/within a shared range of frequencies and, while
we can tune some of them out, lose some of them, the fact
is everything is speaking. I wonder about all the places
these works of Phoebe's are now on display, what words
they are repeating to those who live with them or encounter
them regularly. At *Body Vessel Clay* curated by Jareh Das
at Two Temple Place in 2022, some works from this series
were featured. I remember being at the opening and a man
boasting about having bought one of the works. I wonder
what it says to him.

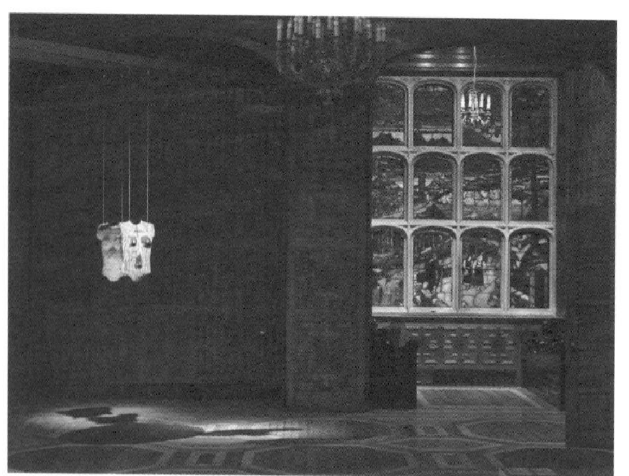

Installation view of
Phoebe Collings-
James, *The subtle rules
the dense* (2022) in
Body Vessel Clay at
Two Temple Place,
London. Photo:
Amit Lennon

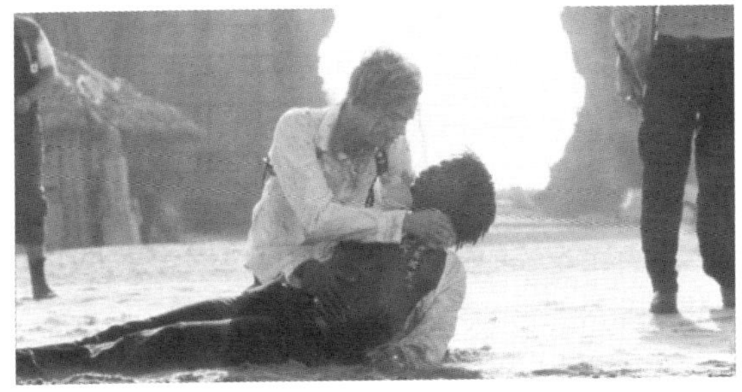

Still from *Romeo + Juliet* (1996). Left to right: Romeo (Leonardo Di Caprio) and Mercutio (Harold Perrineau)

"A plague, o'both your houses!"

These chest plates taunt, I hear them repeating Mercutio's lines - "A plague, o'both your houses!". A cry of anguish, an accusation, a mirror. Dressed up like a jester, exaggerated, elaborated, both strengthening and obscuring the shout, the cry. This is carnival: a fucking plague on both your houses. So many black bodies caught in the crossfire. The armours hang, decorative, louder than 'good taste', a reminder, caught there in mid-air.

"Ay, ay, a scratch, a scratch; marry, 'tis enough."

NOTE TO A FUTURE SELF, AN ARTWORK IN MOTION, HORSE

Rehana Zaman

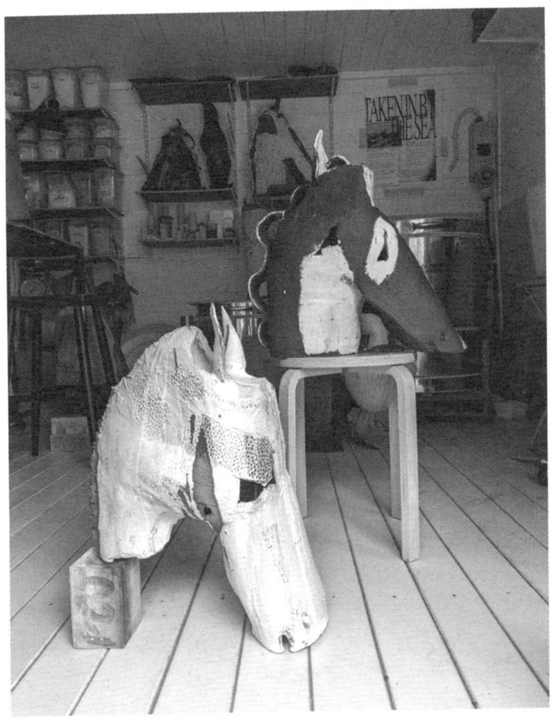

1. A high camp inter-lude following the camera, out of body and distanciated; a side eye to the excess of bad taste and effeminacy. A queer eye on a queer eye, the horse head, a cauterising agent. A rupture to cinematic constructs of heightened and heady machismo. 'Aye, aye, a scratch! a scratch!' Harold Perrineau clutches his abdomen and staggers away, resur-facing incarcerated as Augustus Hill in Oz only to be Lost as Michael Dawson.

Intruder against palatial marble corridors //Interior crane shot// slow and steady //dissolve, sound// laughter and festivities from the wedding party just past, to - silence. //close up// gold sheets, luxuriating kitsch screaming new money mafia opulence. Grey quiff //reveal// a streak of blood, another and more, and all. Scarlet wetness on sheets pulled back, all gold everything, black sateen two piece, brocade edging. Birthing nightmare. //POV// Eyes upturned, milky. A prop? The real deal. Served on ice, between the sheets. Nudged by a big toe.[1] An erotic cadav-erous encounter or (*there's a horse head in my bed*)

Despite the widespread belief that the word 'nightmare' has its origin in horses, its true provenance is thought to derive from the Middle English, *mare*, referring to a female demon that sits on a person's chest when sleeping, seducing, devouring, suffocating, succubus. Lilith: Goddess of sexual liberation and disobedience, transcending the bonds of social reproduction. The false etymology of the horse head persists, bad dreams and the alluring destructiveness of divine feminine power. To be confronted with the stuff of nightmares has a peculiar enthralling magic.

The Subtle Rules the Dense.

The power to displace the 'thing' from its signifying context, for it to accumulate meaning through both the (time) space that has been created around it and the conjuring that sites it otherwise. What is a talisman? An object that imbues the wearer with protective power. Horse heads and torsos are felt through the eyes, the ears, tongues and fingers as breastplates and bascinets. Harbingers of doom and war, love and guardianship. *And I will always love you, I will always love you.*[2]

2. Houston, W. (1992) *I Will Always Love You. The Bodyguard - Original Soundtrack Album*, 1992.

The torso is placed before me, hung on the wall. I place my hands on the waist to meet a lover or loved one. Hands placed either side of midriff, are we stood? Or am I straddling? The precursor to an embrace. The precursor to the meeting of lips.
I lift my son's slight frame from the bed, hands placed either side of midriff, sneaking an embrace as I coerce him towards the bathroom.

We have created them from a sticky clay[3]

3. *Quran, Surah 37 verse 11*

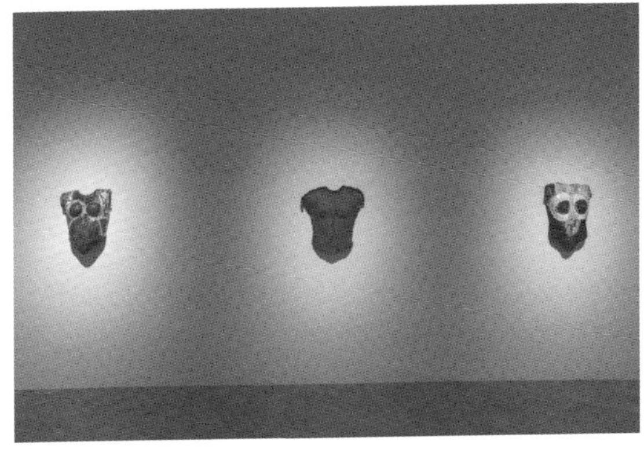

Fingers unfurl into the ground. The immersion of skin into cool dampness, meeting bacteria, enzymes to restore me, give me life please, remind me of my place in the world, praying; close to the ground, honouring those who have held close to the ground before me. Under duress and otherwise…

THE SOIL in Walthamstow is clay laden – 'heavy soil' – difficult to manage, fertile if handled 'the right way'. I arrive here in May 2020 at the height of lockdown to an 80ft garden of horsetail, crumbling tarpaulin, Wray & Nephew miniatures and nitrous oxide canisters. Libations from a time before. Plants are dug. Bay; *for oracular visions, prophetic clarity,* Solanum; *for febrifuge,* Crocosmia/Undwendweni; *for infertility,* Erigeron; *for colds and coughs.* Foreign roots welcome. Embraced and satiated.

A hand fashions and sculpts, giving form to an amorphous mass. The heaving and shifting of weight behind weight that pre-empts my encounter. The lofty hand of production – shaping, moulding – a transference object, a rare breed in the land of outsourced forms where production is so often

happening elsewhere, a displaced economy of wage labour
that sits outside the sanctity of the art world transactions.
I'm revelling in the intimacy of a thing made here, a cord
between the I and the not I that I feel through and am fed.

My lateness lends an adrenaline rush to the cycle, pausing
at Hollow Ponds to soak up swathes of luminescent,
lilac-blue chicory. A half postcode leads past the house I
anticipate entering to the wooded path peeling off the main
road into the forest. Phoebe is at the far end, guiding me
over a fallen tree (was there a storm in the night?) through
a side door that opens up to a suburban back garden and
shed. Two polished steel cylinders – one big and one small
(electric kilns, I come to know), powders stacked in plastic
tubs and jars (for colour or surface variation, I don't know),
horse heads and a clay torso threaded with orange polypro-
pylene. I recognise the work from September 2021 from the
white room, in Camden. One amongst how many casings
flanking two walls of the gallery, three bell like structures
hanging from the ceiling, three bowls gazing upwards from
the floor, caught in a winding black decking rope. A tiled
ceramic on the third wall of the space. Phoebe reminds
me of the sounds, reflected by gloss, dampened by matt,
sinking between the gaps. I couldn't remember.

I remember.
emerging from months of isolation. To fill my heart with
loved ones and colleagues, to manage the deep anxiety
of being, in proximity to others. The desire to disappear
quickly. Dancing some, awkwardly.

I LUV U U U, I LUV U U U, I LUV U U U, I LUV U, U [4]

4. Rascal, D. (2003),
*I Luv U. Boy in Da
Corner*, 2003

I remember.

entering the gallery, a chapel, reaching into calm and quiet, soothed. Meeting one body and another, a breastplate, a chest, take a breath, ribcage rise and fall. In through the nose and release, mouth open, cleansing breath. Regulation. Exhale. Both tender and guarded, each figure poised and redundant in its resting place on the wall.

... my body's calling you,
I'm having so much fun with you
now it's just me and you,
your body's my party, let's get it started, ohhh[5]

The lacquered surface acts as container for line and tone, chaos and restraint. A wet pool disclosing an embodied geography of place and spirit, streaks and glyphs and indentations whispering coded messages.

'For now we see through a glass, darkly; but then face to face: now I know in part; but then shall I know even as also I am known' [6]

~~~~~~

When clay is wet, it plasticizes and its loose form gives way to a soundscape. Snare drums energise and a singular trumpet (or alto sax) leads my ear down avenues and dead ends. Do I know this excerpt, is it a sample left intact or looped to incongruity? An approximation of Ghosts or Spirits?[7] Melodic and mournful gives way to ecstatic revelry and the return of marching bands. The virtuosity of majorettes twizzling batons between kicks and drops in tasselled lycra. A transatlantic call and response, interrupted by a fly?

A bee?

5. Ciara (2013), *Body Party*. Ciara, 2013.

6. 1 Corinthians 13:12, King James Bible

7. Ayler, A (1975) *Ghosts, Ghosts*, 1975. Ayler, A (1966) *Spirits, Spirits*, 1966.
~~~~~~

I'm digressing to a dream where a wasp is stuck in my right ear and a bee in my left. I tip my head to the side shifting my hair which allows the wasp to escape but the bee remains trapped. Its soft fur felt inside my ear canal as it somersaults trying to find a way out. I'm frightened it will burrow deeper into my head and find its way into my brain. Refrains and loops. An assemblage, miscellanea, that oscillate between moments of clarity and opacity.

Hey, changed your hair

Fragments anchored by card pulls, the performative speech of a reading folding back and forth across a year; Judgement, Death, The Empress, The Hermit, The Fool, The Hanged Man, The Star, The Tower. *Audacity leads the way and I follow dutifully in its wake. Stillness is no longer an option.*[8] I hear Phoebe speak and I want to ask who was the one that loved you first, the one you ignored and how did Derek lead you there? My questions give way to the sea. The sound leaks beyond the four walls of the gallery and are encountered in an elsewhere, a residual mess that continues to stir up and dig deep. I put on my headphones and go for a walk.

8. Collings-James, P (2021) *Joy Comes with the Morning,* available at https:// soundcloud.com/ phoebe-collings- james, accessed 9th August 2023

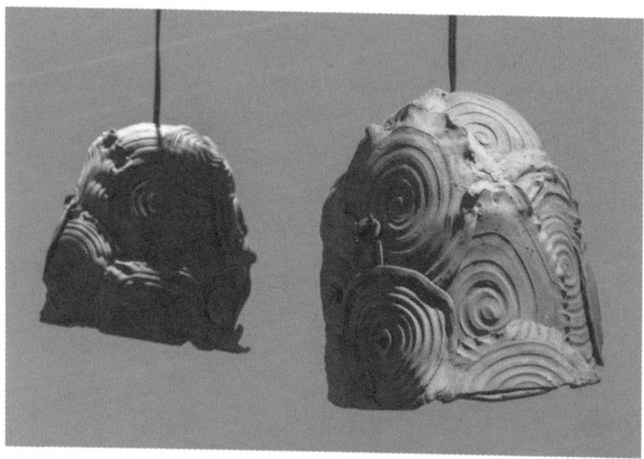

Phoebe Collings- James, Joy Comes With The Morning, 2021 (detail). Photo: Rob Harris

9. Katherine
Mckittrick speaking
on the cyclical
structure of the M/
Nourbse Phillips'
Zong! McKittrick, K.
(2015) 'Diachronic
Loops/Deadweight
Tonnage/Bad Made
Measure,' The Cultural
Geographies Annual
Lecture, 2015.

10. Ibid.

I am signalling how this creative text, if read through the lens of black life, offers up a diachronic loop that undoes biocentric logic by looking in on it and demanding the reader contend with the ability for this logic to sustain itself.[9]

One must work hard to make sense of the words, locutions, and voices in order to envision the bigger conceptual picture that turns back on itself...[10]

END NOTE FOR PAST AND FUTURE SELVES. A CARD PULL TO END CARD PULLS. HORSE

//A white horse outlined in blues, pinks and purple. A parted fringe and a look coquettish. Personal power can be accessed when the horse shows up, sexual energy and companionship. Collaborate with the situation, let it take you further than you could on your own//.[11]

11. Kroll. M. (2017),
Nature Nurture Oracle
Deck.

PHOEBE COLLINGS-JAMES IN CONVERSATION WITH KATHRYN YUSOFF

In Spring 2023, Phoebe Collings James was invited by Beaconsfield to be an Environmental Artist in Residence, joining the nationwide museum project *The Wild Escape*, to explore the multifaceted meanings of the term 'sustainability'. Linked, as a part of their residency, Phoebe spoke to Professor Kathryn Yusoff about her 2019 book *A Billion Black Anthropocenes or None*. The following is an edited transcript of that conversation.

PCJ *Let's start with talking about your book,* A Billion Black Anthropocenes or None.

We first met, I believe, in 2021 when we were on a panel together, at the Whitechapel Gallery, called Terra Firma: The Politics of Earth. *There were four of us, talking about the earth from very different angles; I was talking about clay, rock and the earth as I relate to it as an artist and you were speaking about your book.*

It took me until last summer to read it and, when I finally did, I packed it in a bag with me when I went to the Archie Bray Ceramics Residency in Montana, in the US.

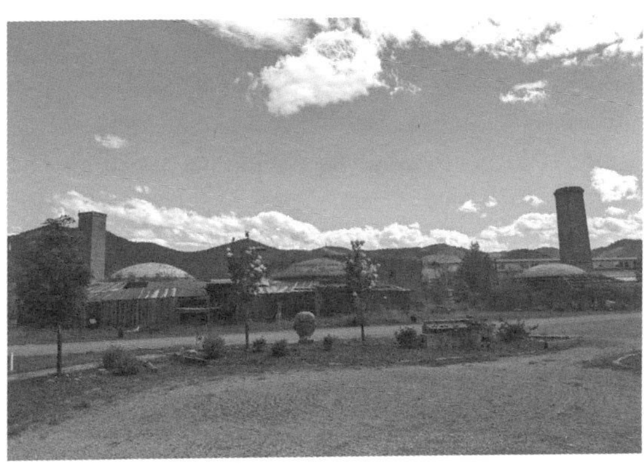

Afro Mingei Institute studio intensive at The Archie Bray Foundation for the Ceramic Arts, Montana, 2022. Photo: Phoebe Collings-James

I'd had an instinct that it was going to be the right moment to read it, with all of the histories of the gold rush town – the legacies of indigenous people who were murdered and the land that was stolen and the Black people that helped rebuild it – and with the mountains surrounding every single view. But also being there and making ceramics, in a way making molten rocks, really brought your book to life for me.

I wanted to start with a question from the reading group that we held here at Beaconsfield a month ago. Everyone who attended had something really personal to say about how it had affected them, or what they took away from it, so it's a question that came from many different angles: Who is this book for? And how has it been received and used since its publication?

KY It's a great question. It started very much as an academic intervention in a set of debates that I was involved in, as a geographer, with scientists and with social scientists about the anthropocene. Often I found myself to be the only racialised person, and often the only woman, in the room. So it started from my feeling that these debates about the future of the earth seemed to include only a very small sample in terms of representation. But, alongside this, I was also working on a much longer project, which was looking at the history of geology. What I found in geologic archives in the course of the project was kind of shocking to me but it really shouldn't have been; that comes from being immersed in an environmental geographic education that doesn't put together these connections.

So it started out as a book for white geologists and geographers and the very imperial subject of geography. But, while I was reading a lot of Black feminist work and trying to work out how to grapple with these earth archives, I started

writing it towards a different community, which wasn't
necessarily my own in terms of my academic background,
rather toward what I think of as a Black feminist ethic. One
centred around seeing the very subjective and embodied
relations of the earth and of politics while really trying to
reckon with the archive and the absences and erasures
within it.

PCJ *I wonder if it's useful to include here the blurb about
the book, just to bring some context to the conversation.*

> *No geology is neutral, writes Kathryn Yusoff. Tracing
> the colour line of the Anthropocene, A Billion Black
> Anthropocenes or None examines how the grammar of
> geology is foundational to establishing the extractive
> economies of subjective life and the earth under colo-
> nialism and slavery. Yusoff initiates a transdisciplinary
> conversation between black feminist theory, geography,
> and the earth sciences, addressing the politics of the
> Anthropocene within the context of race, materiality,
> deep time, and the afterlives of geology.*

*I wonder if you could expand on what the Anthropocene
refers to in this context and what your writing in this book is
against or in relation to?*

KY At the time I began writing in 2015, the Anthropocene
was a term that had only recently been coined to capture
the geomorphic effects of humans on the earth, on all
the major earth systems, and how that might map onto
questions of climate change and earth futures. Amongst
geologists, there was a race to name the origin story of the
anthropocene, when it began. It was fueled by a specific
concern with endings and the state of humanity; there were
a number of suggestions around the atomic era, the begin-

ning of industrialisation and some suggestions around what was often referred to as the Columbian 'exchange', which was a euphemism for colonialism.

Amongst this race to name the 'golden spike' of the anthropocene – which is the geologic term for staking an origin claim – I was more interested in thinking about the flesh of geology: what was the corporal reality of these spikes; who had to experience these impacts; who bore these experiences, these events? I wanted to scrape away some of the layers around those languages of materiality and, as an example, to think about the impact of atomic testing on indigenous people, to understand these spikes as inhabited places, inhabited parts of the earth.

What you find at the centre of these suggestions for the origins of the anthropocene, time and time again, is a racialised event; race is a dynamic in those impacts and falls disproportionately on Black and brown people, particularly through colonialism. So, as a way to help us identify how to move forward, I really wanted to get to a place where we could see that the anthropocene is not the anthropocene but the anthropocene is colonialism.

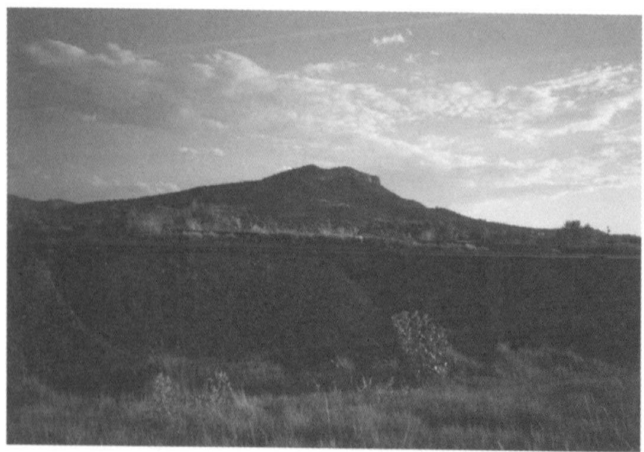

View of the train tracks by The Archie Bray Foundation for the Ceramic Arts, Montana, 2022. Photo: Phoebe Collings-James

One of the key things that happened in colonialism was the industrialisation of property as a quality of subjectivity in enslavement. That relationship between who gets to own property and who is instead treated as property, and its ongoing legacy — for example, in South Africa around landlessness and labour — is crucial to what becomes thought of as the anthropocene. That's a fracture from land that is experienced in very different ways. That's something to bear in mind when we think about the effects of property.

PCJ *I feel a bit cautious about the idea that a severed relationship to the land is the root of some of these issues we've been discussing. To me, it's one of the problematic things that come up in terms of the climate crisis. These things can't be separated very neatly within us. I think colonialism is a really important example of that because, thinking particularly of the height of the British Empire, both land and people were being so violently disrespected in one place at the same time as the realisation of the bucolic landscape in the UK. They created some of the most beautiful parks and gardens while developing huge personal wealth and personal relationships to botany, ecology and geology, all through the subjugation of British and colonial subjects.*

KY Exactly, the profits from plantations in Jamaica transformed Scotland; a third of the land in Scotland was turned into stately homes because people wanted to demonstrate the wealth they'd accumulated from Jamaican plantations and to have a place to go shooting on the weekend. We have to think about these interlocking systems. We can think about the plantation or the strip mine as a way of stripping the soil, people and the landscape and how it was those mines and plantations that built stately homes, because that was how you demonstrated that wealth. I think the question is about how we challenge some of these values and what word we can use that stands against "natural resources" and the naturalisation of continued extraction.

PCJ *Could you maybe say why you put quotation marks around natural? I'm often thinking about this idea of what's natural and that nature itself might not be a given.*

KY Absolutely, I'd put quotation marks not just around the natural but around resources as well. I think they're some of the most slippery words in the English language. This is something I was trying to get across by using the term 'white geology', that the legacy of colonialism was the transformation of the earth using the grammars of 'natural resources'. 'White geology' and the history of those geologic practices is multiethnic now. It's global; in terms of nation states, everyone is participating in really extreme forms of extraction.

That's being naturalised and it's becoming very difficult to intervene in the assumptions around those practices and the assumptions around the 'naturalness' of extraction as the basis of geopolitical life.

PCJ *I really appreciate the connections you make because they allowed me to condense all of these ideas that had been circling in my head about artists—mostly white artists, in my opinion—who dealt with the anthropocene in their work. These were the first times I'd heard that word in a space or a language that I have some understanding of; art practice, art objects, and material forms. I'd been considering this disconnection between earth and materials, but I felt like there was a tendency to approach the anthropocene with a disconnection from the reality of art making and not with any kind of material grounding. Working with ceramics,* *that disconnection is there, knowing that most of the materials I was using have been mined or quarried, and how those present day and historic processes require people whose bodies endure a lot of stress and sickness to get those materials out.*

For me, at times, it felt like quite a visceral bodily assault to re-read and re-remember the degradation that was suffered by my ancestors in the Caribbean and many people across the Americas. I was wondering how it was for you to write about slavery and the commodification of black people.

KY What to do with archives of violence is a difficult question. I'm not a Black subject, that doesn't land on my body in the same way. Geography is a very imperial discipline and the discourse around enslavement in the UK is very sanitised. Often it just trades in these euphemisms and a language that cleans colonialism of its embodied toll. I wanted to acknowledge the cost of these geographic imaginations, the way they landed in flesh. The abstractions of a scientific quest (as the battle to name the Anthropocene became), refused the embodiment of those events, as actual events that had a human cost (the atomic tests, the invasion of the Americas, the Industrial Revolution and its links to enslavement and diaspora). These are dangerous abstractions when you are talking about the future. If earth futures are explicitly in play and the game is all about naming, then we must ask about what a name carries, what words are made to do and hold and what words never get spoken.

While writing *A Billion Black Anthropocenes or None*, I was trying to tread the very difficult line between acknowledging the viscerality of those long histories and considering the effect that might have on readers, because those are not histories that have gone away. For example, I just cycled down the A2 and that tells you everything you need to know about how air pollution disproportionately impacts black and brown bodies; these are very current and very embodied events. In *A Billion Black Anthropocenes or None*, I'm trying to enflesh this geology and to show the intimacies and forced intimacies of what it means to be situated within colonial extractive economies, basically, whilst being cautious around revisiting violence and how that might land today.

I think, in a very straightforward way, I wanted to talk about violence, because I think violence is missing in a lot of our debates about colonialism and about race. If race in the US is very overdescribed, I think, in the UK, it's very underdescribed. There's a studied politeness that avoids talking about race because it makes people uncomfortable which, to me, seems like a good reason to centre the issue. But I understand that that will also be experienced very differently for readers.

I wanted to find a place to talk about violence mindful of the trauma of that violence (and how that is experienced and directed at blackness) without re-activating that violence in ways of writing that sanitised or sensationalised it. There is also much more violence in the archive that I didn't and still haven't talked about. There is a line of trespass when we talk about directed violence that is not our own. And there is a violence to that act of talking about forms of degradation that are not our direct experience of the world, but at the same time, I am in a geography department and I have a responsibility to work through those deadly inheritances of this most colonial of all subjects.

PCJ *Rocks come up again and again in your book and also the idea of geologic life. Could you expand on this idea of geologic life and talk about the flesh you have given in the book to the rock matter?*

KY We're very used to thinking of ourselves as biologic subjects; we can think about the biologisms of our body but we're very unused to thinking about ourselves as mini-earth systems or forms of geologic assemblages. We tend to think of subjectivity as political, as cultural, as biological but not as geological. In putting together this idea of geologic life, I wanted to force a reckoning with the inhuman and really to acknowledge the geologic composition of our bodies. It's thinking of geology as a first state that bodies come out of; the very possibility of biology is, in a relational sense, entirely reliant on the earth. I wanted to focus on geologic life and to encourage people to think of ourselves as participating in the earth, not just through damage, but actually in intimate ways, that we actually engage with and ingest.

But also thinking about the histories of these geologies as configuring certain kinds of bodies in certain kinds of ways; we're all here because of fossil fuels, for example, but equally the geotrauma of colonialism scars the bones of the enslaved and that has a generational set of effects and epigenetic effects. The different geologies that we participate with are held in the body and they're held in the body in different kinds of ways. If we think about this in terms of prolonging life, for example, we can think about where I work in East London; in Tower Hamlets, the life expectancy is ten years less than in The City and that's configured around very material forms of racialised experience. I just really wanted to centre life as a geologic fact but also think about geology and racial equality.

PCJ *I'm wondering why now, or why at the point when you started the research? What was your geography/geology life like? Was it a linear trajectory or was it informed by a new urgency?*

KY 20 years ago, I did my PhD in the Antarctic and I was really into thinking about the continent as a place without any indigenous population. I was really interested in the idea that there were no subjects there but actually, as soon as you get down to the Antarctic, you realise that it's intensely social and political.

But the very particular swerve I had in my own relationship to environmental studies and geography was when I was looking at oil and gas in California. It was the summer of the first set of very high profile police killings in 2014 and I ended up spending a good part of my time in Los Angeles, just being on the streets in protest. I was having a racial education on the streets of LA, and an education about the police. It took a while but I started to put those things together, to put together gas and oil infrastructures and extraction with questions of race and its geophysics. Like in 'Black Lives Matter', it's about matter. It took a while to learn how to think that way, within the institutions and histories of thought that I'd been involved in, but my research and my book is the outcome of that process of thinking or trying to think more expansively about that relation between material and racial worlds. I think it was about getting an education on the streets of LA.

PCJ *One thing that is really prominent in the book is the amount of quotes, and brilliant quotes, from Black feminist thought, specifically pulling out quotes that relate to rocks. I'm going to read some of them and I thought it would be good if you could talk about them a bit further so:*

1. Edouard Glissant, *Poetic Intention*, 1969. English translation by Nathalie Stephens, 2010.

2. Dionne Brand, *In Another Place, Not Here*, 1996.

3. Kathryn Yusoff, *A Billion Black Anthropocenes or None*, 2018.

4. Ibid.

5. Aimé Cesaire, *Return to My Native Land*, 1956.

I build my language with rocks[1]

I want to go against the ground, grind it in my teeth, but most I want to plunge my hands in stone[2]

And there is a need to desediment the social life of geology, to place it in the terror of its coercive acts and the interstitial moments of its shadow geology—what I call a billion Black Anthropocenes[3]

of the flesh that hews the rock, that plants the sugar plantation, that blasts and gets blasted in the mines, that transports and carries the pathogens and pollutions of those Spikes as processes of destratifications[4]

Red earth, blood earth, blood brother earth[5]

KY That's my rock collection! I was interested in rock piles as a method in engaging with the broken earths that colonialism made. To think with rocks as a form of inhuman memory, in which rocks could be collectors of stories, disobedience, oaths, a medium of temporality that exceeds colonialism.

PCJ *I actually have a much longer list than this but I picked out some that particularly spoke to me.*

KY A lot of those writers, particularly Edouard Glissant, Patrick Chamoiseau, Césaire, Fanon, Sylvia Winter, are trying to create a political language of subjectivity, of the landscape, out of the geotrauma of being coercively transported to a place and trying to have a relationship with its landscape. There seems to be a real investment in rocks and I think that's why there are so many rock stories; we get rock stories in Nina Simone's song 'Sinnerman' and

James Baldwin's story about rock piles. I think in these
stories and songs we see a methodology for building things
out of rocks, out of fragments, out of broken earths.

I was really interested in this method as an alternative to
traditional geographies; if you think about colonial western
geographic imaginations — of the earth, of the globe —
they're very macro views that come from above. What it
means to make your language out of rocks, as Glissant talks
about, is a methodology of starting from below with the very
broken things in the earth and seeing a kind of allyship there.
So I think those writers offer a different kind of materiality
that can be part of a new language to consider what it means
to inhabit the earth under these incredibly violent conditions.

Younger scholars are doing a lot of excellent work in really
trying to think through the historic relations to geology as
well as the political implications of those relationships. I
think there's a move to really, even within museum collec-
tions, to think about rocks as colonial artefacts, not just
rocks. You go into a natural history museum and there's the
history of the earth on one side, there's gems and minerals,
and then there's life; those things are separated and they're
never brought together. I think some of the larger move-
ments around colonisation are really trying to grapple with
these separations. That's why interdisciplinary work matters
in the sense that it can begin to show us how these things
join up and what the bigger picture is.

I find it really optimistic — and I'm not usually given to opti-
mism — that we may look to the cosmos and the earth for a
set of philosophies, a set of ways to live, and a set of ways
to think that can help us escape these carceral conditions
and provide a new politics of subjectivity. So that's why I've
been collecting rock stories and rock parables; because I

think they're doing something very political in redescribing a new geographic imagination of the earth.

And also when you start to look for rocks, they pop up all over the place. In soil, rocks, mounds, pottery, black-smithing, gritty residues of counter-archives can be found, that cling to the world in its erasure. I like the idea of the earth as a collector of disobedience, rebellion, and revolt, claiming time outside the colonial clock. The earth imagined as an archival medium, alongside bodies and ground that carry the aftershocks of colonialism as geotrauma is also a site of methodological redress—building spaces of remem-brance, talking with ghosts and shifting temporalities in the colonial afterlives.

PCJ *As we talk, I'm looking at the brick walls outside Beaconsfield Gallery and thinking about how, in a way, the ceramic process of going to liquid heat and then returning to a cold solid, makes brick technically a kind of molten rock. And in turn, it makes me think of concrete and stories about things emerging from the cracks, whether in Tupac lyrics or the works of other artists who have explored what it means to live in the concrete metropolis as a different type of rock.*

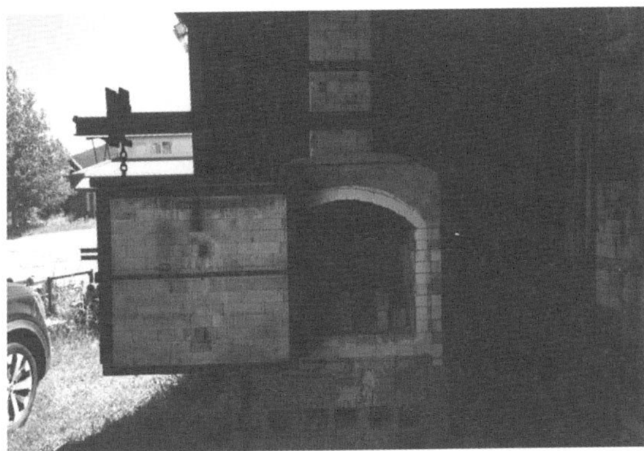

A brick kiln at The Archie Bray Founda-tion for the Ceramic Arts, Montana, 2022. Photo: Phoebe Collings-James

KY These inhuman engagements are also framed for me by the question of "How to have a rock in the family" that works against colonial divisions of life and non-life, and all the other genealogies that don't prioritise propertied inheritance or heteronormative patriarchal ideas of family and sexuality.

PCJ *Can you say more? In what ways?*

KY What enlightenment and then colonialist discourse does is separate nature and culture; having a rock in the family is a way to undo a lot of those histories of thought and genealogy. It goes back to what I was trying to say about biology tending towards normativity, particularly in the historic ways in which the family has been imagined, and in terms of material practices of extraction. So having a rock in the family is one way to think about how you might disrupt those things and terms and release other ways of imagining kinship and belonging.

PCJ *Who is the rock? What is it?*

KY The non-human world. Something that hits you on the head, if you are unfortunate. The inhuman world is not outside of the possibilities of our being so, if we have a rock in the family, we have a different set of ethical obligations or commitments to the earth. It's a lot easier to do with non-humans, like pets and animals, than it is with rocks.

PCJ *It brings to my mind what happens to people who are perceived as 'the rock of the family' and in turn how they might be treated as being unbreakable and not having the same needs as others. That relationship can be a kind of othering, or isolating.*

KY You're right. When you consider the numerous recent studies on black pain and the medical codification of black pain, which is not properly acknowledged in the healthcare system, leading to a projection of an inhuman quality onto certain people's bodies and a non-recognition of suffering.

You remind me to read against that inhuman subjectivity and to consider ways in which we can think about creative intimacies with the inhuman that are not so deadly, that are not all about subjection and violence. I think that's what the enslaved certainly did in the practice of marronage and other discrete forms of environmental practices. I also wanted to give some space and language to those resistances and craft practices.

PCJ *Returning to your point about stories, I'm reminded of one of the last audio recordings I made of two of my great-aunts, Ellen and Beryl, talking in Jamaica. I'm not sure what the bigger point of the story was but, from what I understood, they were basically talking about some rocks in the local landscape and how they had moved from the time they were kids until when I was speaking to them at ages 78 and 90; the movement of the rocks had shifted the way the water ran and the route they had to take from one place to another. I was in and out of the kitchen and had this recording running while I was doing other things and, when I returned to the audio later, I was really curious as to why this had come up; the people in this story didn't seem that visible to me but remembering these routes and these surfaces and themselves in relation to it seemed to be evoking a lot of conversation between them. Maybe it's just evoking this sense of land and movement and aliveness.*

KY Yes, and we make our stories with an inhuman world, it's both a substance of flesh but also an orientation.

Are you thinking of doing anything with those rocks? Or are they just sitting there?

PCJ *At the time, in 2016, I included the recording in a sound piece titled* Primordial Soup *which was exhibited in New York. There was an interesting psychic convergence of three isles, UK, Jamaica and NY (where I was living). I also created a poster for the show that had the conversation - a poem[6] - overlaid on a photograph from Jamaica of a large generator subsumed by the wet growth of the forest. So, the rocks are already coming in.*

I got to travel to Cornwall last year to visit some of the old mines there, which gave me the chance to better understand how things like kaolin are extracted from granite and be more aware of the materials that I've been using and how they relate to rock in more direct ways. The rock doesn't exist in a vacuum — it is in relation to water, air and people and touch. There are these whole processes around it that can't be isolated.

I think that understanding, when I come back into my very contemporary electric-powered studio in London with very conveniently packaged materials from Bath Potters, gives me a different concept of what I'm using and how the forms I'm making might relate to all the things I'm thinking about, particularly in relation to black feminist thought and my own personhood.

KY One of the things that I've been really trying to think more about recently is inhuman memory. In the work of a lot of those Caribbean writers, rocks are a part of the story

6. *Rock - A Conversation in Jamaica*, pg. 82

and they hold memories — they hold the memory of the Caribs and the escaped slaves. They are these sentinels for telling the cacophonous and capricious histories that are not represented in the museum. If we think about statues as one rock embodiment of history — with the need to pull a lot of those statues down — and the museum as this colonial storehouse often of looted objects, what other objects, like the rocks of your great-aunts' story, are there that hold stories of people that have been erased and people whose stories are not told in statues or the museum? That's why I try to think about rocks not just as a part of a history but also as a place to gather when 'surface politics' don't allow those stories to be told. We can almost think about those rocks as an underground that's overground, an underground set of stories that needs to be surfaced, but with care.

What is the capacity of the earth to potentiate shared social and racialized histories against a history of the 'inhuman' that had a central role in organising racializing and racist subjectivities and perpetuating colonial infrastructures that continue to subjugate black and brown life? Can rocks instruct on stories of erasure, if not the erased and forgotten? Does the earth remember more than it forgets? Does it hold what is forgotten?

PCJ *It brings to mind Beverly Buchanan's* Marsh Ruins; *she was an artist who was based in Macon, Georgia and worked a lot with stone and tabby concrete, a type of concrete made of burnt oyster shells.* Marsh Ruins *was a work where she created several big boulder-like rocks in the marshes, which were intentionally not particularly easy to get to or find. They would become more or less visible and sometimes disappear in the water with the tide. I also wonder, with this whole storytelling idea, how artists tell*

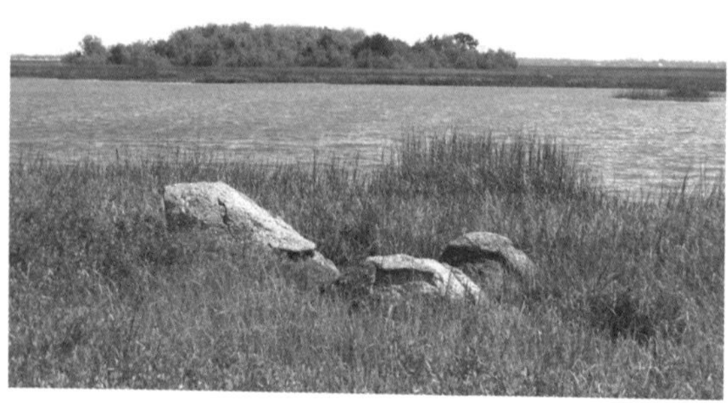

those stories through making things and interventions,
especially ones outside of museums.

KY One of the real joys of this book, in its very cheap
packable form, is that it has led to a lot of collaborations
with artists. The title of the book 'A Billion Black Anthropocenes or None' is about both the Billion and the None as a
wager and as a provocation for all sorts of stories and histories that are not necessarily mine to tell. It's been fantastic
to see how the provocation leads to all kinds of different
ways of thinking about the earth and thinking about these
long embedded stories that don't often get told.

The book was written as a very particular thing and, since
publications, it's had this whole other life. When you put
something out in the world, particularly when it doesn't
cost very much, it circulates in all sorts of spaces. I've had
really interesting conversations with people like nurses
who are interested in what nursing might look like in the
anthropocene. To me, that's an amazing question; what
does healthcare look like in the anthropocene?

Thinking about the way in which bodies are historically raced and subjugated, it's an amazing question, that's a really thoughtful response.

Geologists are getting there. There's a movement within the geosciences to really take those histories seriously. With geography and geology, they're very traditionally white spaces but that's also changing. Academia is very slow but I think rethinking our relationship to the earth is more of a collective project across lots of different cultural spaces. That's happening everywhere, in lots of different ways, which is great to see.

And, also to be aware of the right to see, the hidden, like Beverly Buchanan's work and its refusal to be monumentalised.

PCJ *Thinking about how deep we are in the shit of capitalism and colonialism, where even the new paths and renewable energies involve scurrying for rare earth materials, using materials that still must undergo extremely labour-intensive processes, brings up a question I often consider in my life and work, which is 'how do we live'? How are we actually going to live through this, to survive through this and potentially even feel good sometimes? How is that going to be possible?*

For a lot of people, that can come through connection and images, poetry, writing, conversations and ways to create culture with each other. That's one way that those things can feel possible and become both very furtive resistance and real resistance in times where everything feels pretty bleak in terms of a lot of the extraction practices we have discussed.

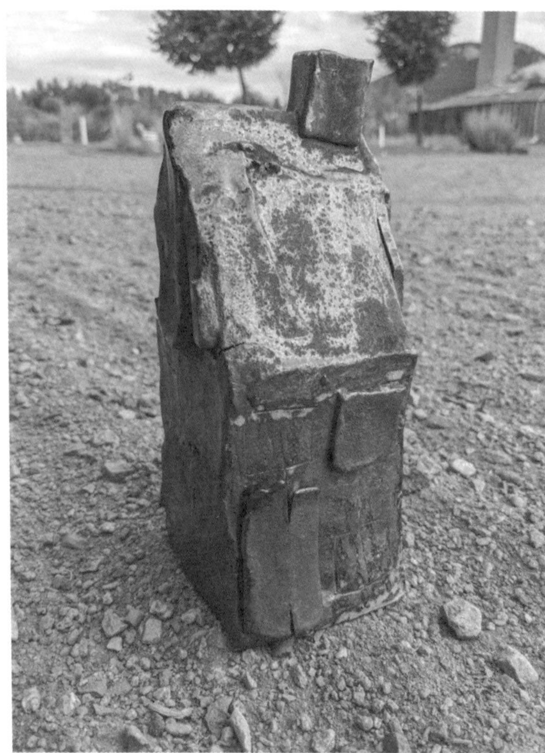

Phoebe Collings-James, *a house for beverly*, 2022. The Archie Bray Foundation for the Ceramic Arts, Montana, USA.

And actually, even thinking about ceramics, most of the materials that I have in the studio, like alumina and different oxides, are only available because they are used in many other industries, from our teeth to computing to toilets, everything. Without that demand, there wouldn't be this little corner of resource that can be allocated to the pottery industry, which despite its extensive size would not be enough for them to put all these systems in place, to mine all these materials.

KY You work a lot with clay and mud, what do those media mean to you?

PCJ *I think a lot about the way the materials feel to touch and also about the knowledge that they can imbue, whether that's teacups, or ceremonial objects, or pot shards from ceramics that have been around for millenia. Firstly, I really enjoy the way they feel and hold heat but also how ceramics turn to rock through this process of intense heat and how analogous that is with igneous and metamorphic rocks that occur in nature.*

And on the other side, I like the story telling of it. I enjoy the fact that, outside of a gallery or museum system, one day these objects might stay for the most part the same as how I created them but maybe end up in a ditch. It's thrilling to me that, even in a broken form, they will give information. I guess I'm excited by that relationship to discarded ceramic objects that have held knowledge, over centuries, over millennia.

Clay is a material that's stable, malleable and tender. To me, it feels like the closest expression of my thinking that I can make, outside of my own body, and offer into a space; to speak some of the things that I would like to speak but I would ever be too shy to or not able to fully articulate with my own voice or flesh. That's mostly what excites me about clay or mud and also what connects it to other elements of my practice, working with performance, working with sound and these very oral and physical acts and interventions.

I went to the Henry Moore Museum in Hertfordshire recently, and there was a really brilliant tour of his house. The person doing the tour was describing how, as a child, Moore used to rub liniments on his mum's back when she came home from work. A lot of his sculptures are based on the shape and

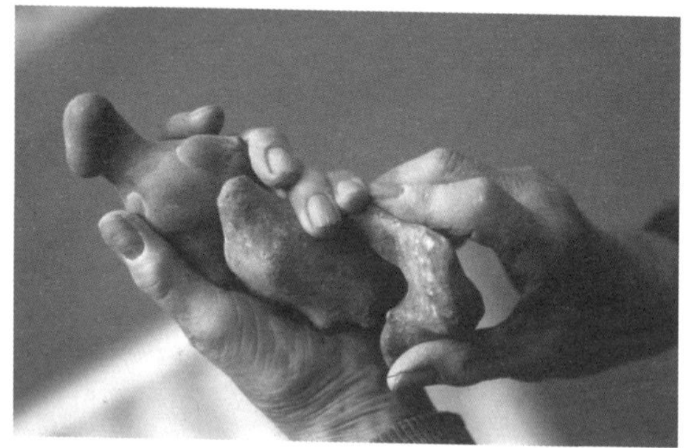

Henry Moore's hands holding found objects in the Bourne Maquette Studio, 2 February 1978. Photo: Gemma Levine, courtesy Gemma Levine, the Henry Moore Estate and the Tate Archive

expanse of her back — I think there is even one where it has her low ponytail. I just think about that idea that he would be sculpting rock and making maquettes with that same touch that he'd had as a kid, doing this very intimate act with his mum. That really brought some of these connections between touch and materials to life for me.

I also often take ceramics home with me and take them to bed, or sit on my sofa and just hold and touch them. I find these materials very seductive. Whether that be staring at a brick wall and becoming engrossed in its patterns, or even living in Victorian housing in London and knowing the buildings are only just staying together but they could also live for another 100 years if you just don't move that one brick. These kinds of things excite me as much as being in the woods or near the ocean or rock or traditionally awe inspiring landscapes.

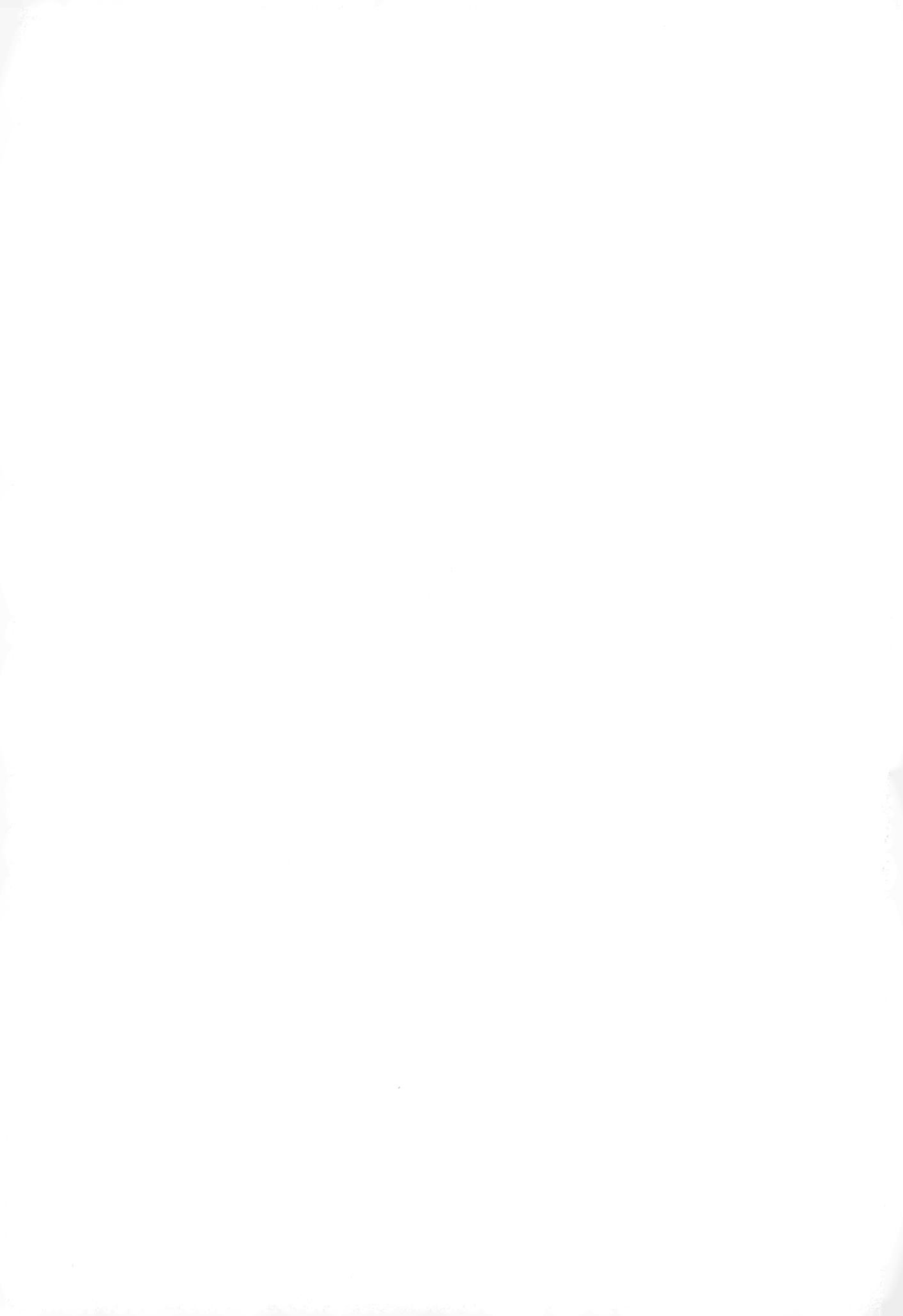

ROCK - A CONVERSATION IN JAMAICA

Aunt Ellen & Aunt Beryl

I don't think that's official
ya know

I think that's people that
are trying to capture it
an doing that

And that is why when
it rains you find that water
comes up off the ground
because

the water is normally
on its way to the sea

I stopped there, i was forced to stop
there because of the rain

and you could see the water
bubbling up in the middle
of the road ya know

because dem block it
from flowing

That is why that area near the rock
it's not even good

Somebody told me that when it
rained, when they were children
that dey would go up there
and hear it

the river like
underneath the rock

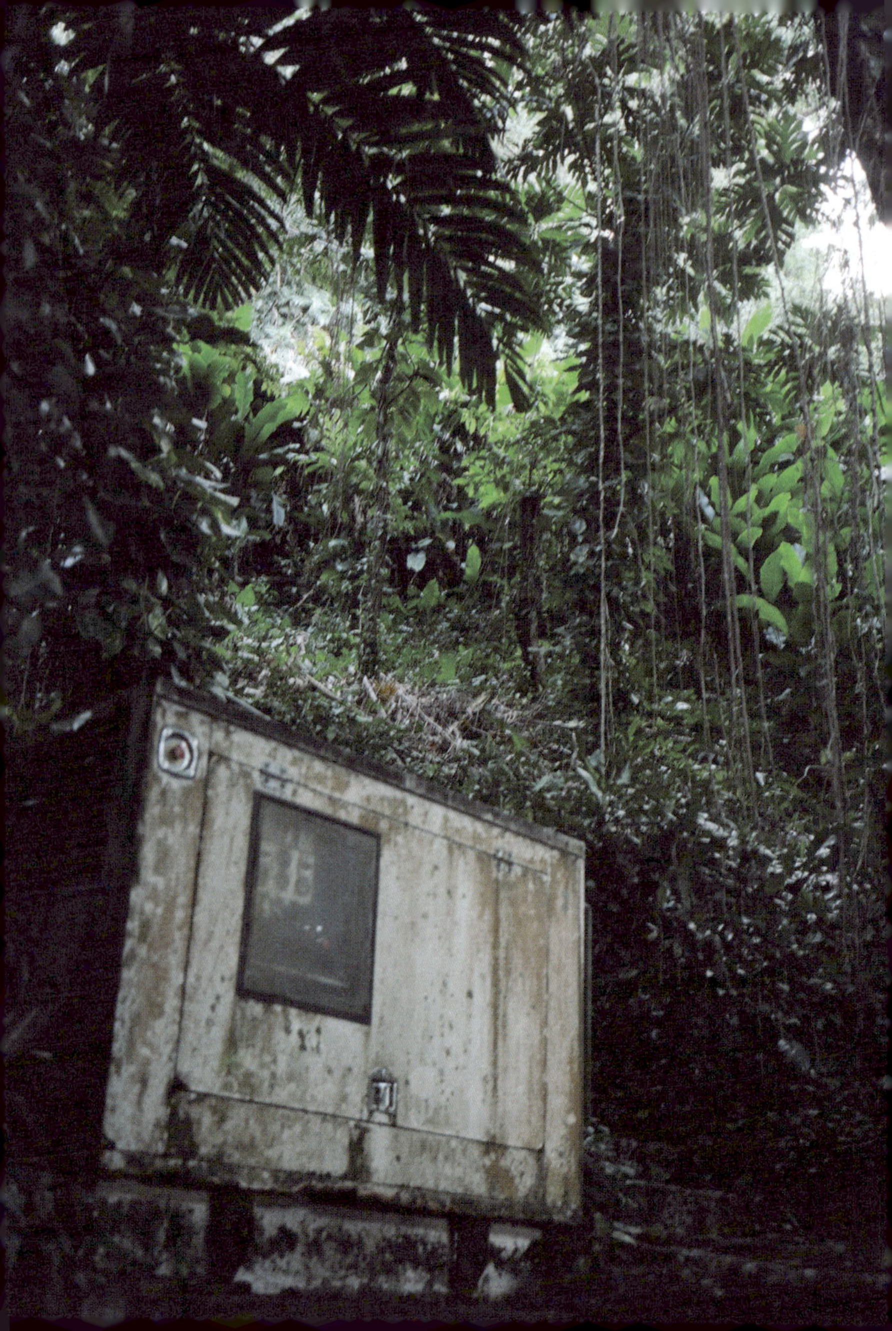

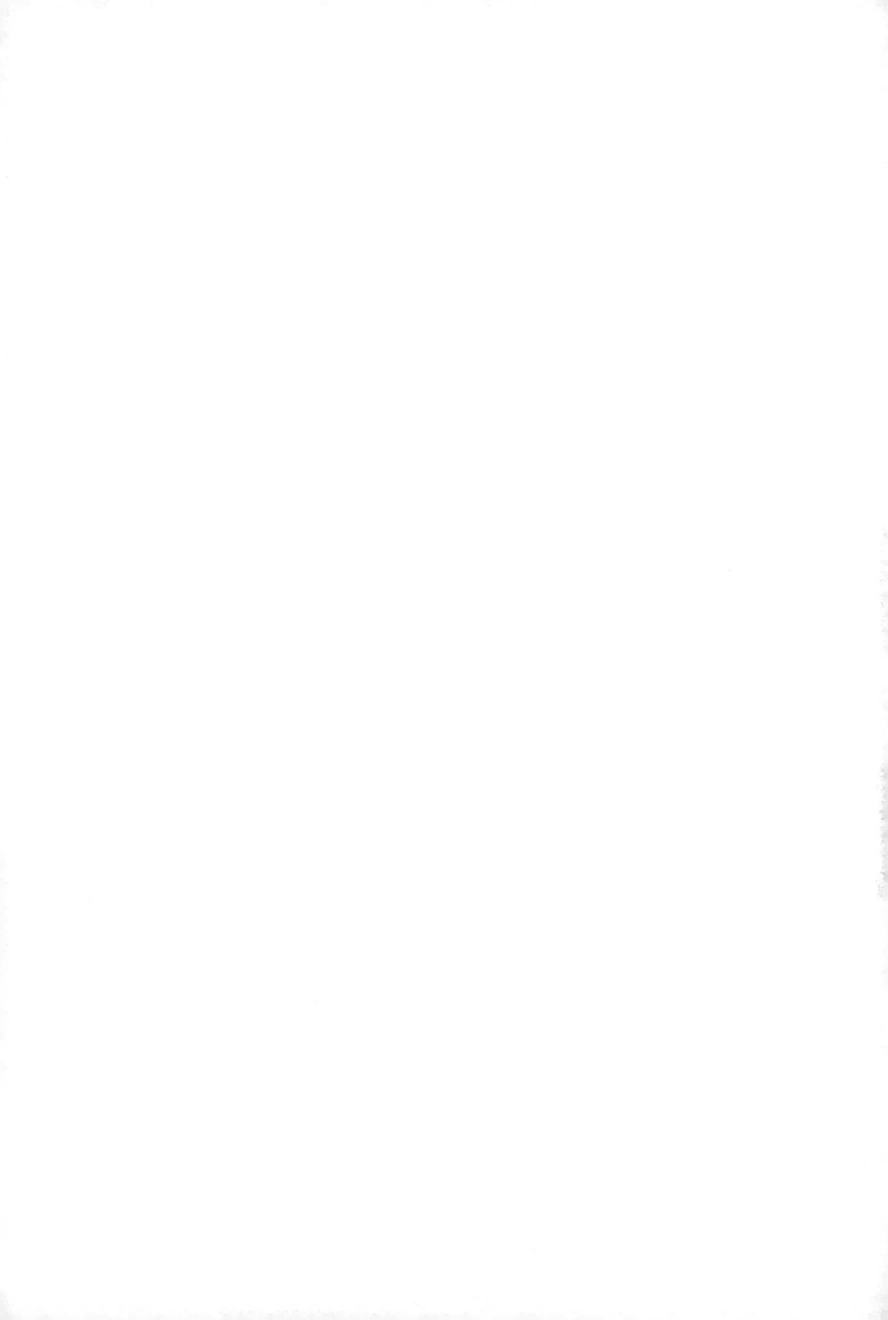

Acknowledgements:

Phoebe Collings-James would like to
thank, Jamila Johnson-Small for their
loving confidants, Nisha Matthew, Martin
Clarke and Sevak Zargarian for their
support during the Freelands Ceramic
Fellowship at Camden Arts Centre where
the first iteration of this work came to life,
Jareh Das's scholarship and friendship,
Helen Walsh & everyone at York Art
Gallery and Two Temple Place, Rózsa
Farkas, Ruth Pilston, Daniella Valz Gen,
Rehana Zaman, Kathryn Yusoff and
Beaconsfield Gallery, Theaster Gates and
all at The Archie Bray who made my time
in Montana so special. Valda, Beryl, Ellen,
Evelyn, Bob, Daisy, Nikki, Jimmy.

Concept: Phoebe Collings-James

Texts: SERAFINE1369, Rehana Zaman, Kathryn Yusoff & Phoebe Collings-James

Photographs on pages 32-35 by Paul Tucker. Courtesy of Two Temple Place.

Additional photography by Tim Bowditch & Rob Harris

Arcadia Missa Publications
35 Duke Street
London
W1U 1LH

www.arcadiamissa.com
@ArcadiaMissa
info@arcadiamissa.com

Arcadia Missa Publications are available from the gallery, our website and selected stockists.

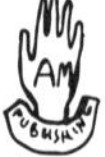